ISBN 978-1-5285-6110-5
PIBN 10931431

1 MONTH OF
FREE
READING

at

www.ForgottenBooks.com

By purchasing this book you are eligible for one month membership to ForgottenBooks.com, giving you unlimited access to our entire collection of over 1,000,000 titles via our web site and mobile apps.

To claim your free month visit:

www.forgottenbooks.com/free931431

English
Français
Deutsche
Italiano
Español
Português

www.forgottenbooks.com

Mythology Photography **Fiction**
Fishing Christianity **Art** Cooking
Essays Buddhism Freemasonry
Medicine **Biology** Music **Ancient**
Egypt Evolution Carpentry Physics
Dance Geology **Mathematics** Fitness
Shakespeare **Folklore** Yoga Marketing
Confidence Immortality Biographies
Poetry **Psychology** Witchcraft
Electronics Chemistry History **Law**
Accounting **Philosophy** Anthropology
Alchemy Drama Quantum Mechanics
Atheism Sexual Health **Ancient History**
Entrepreneurship Languages Sport
Paleontology Needlework Islam
Metaphysics Investment Archaeology
Parenting Statistics Criminology
Motivational

HARRY McMULLAN
Attorney General

WILLIAM B. UMSTEAD
Governor of North Carolina

CHARLES F. CARROLL
State Superintendent of
Public Instruction

A REPORT TO THE GOVERNOR OF NORTH CAROLINA
By Albert Coates and James C. N. Paul

Table of Contents

Part I

THE BACKGROUND OF THE DECISION

I. LETTER OF TRANSMITTAL	1
II. THE NEGRO COMES TO NORTH CAROLINA	1
III. THE FREE NEGRO IN NORTH CAROLINA	4
IV. SCHOOLING FROM 1665 to 1865	4
V. SCHOOLING FROM 1865 to 1954	5
A. Separate Schools in North Carolina	5
B. Separate Schools in Other States	5
C. Progress of Schools in North Carolina under "Separate but Equal Doctrine"	6
D. Actions Speak Louder Than Words	7
VI. COMING EVENTS CAST THEIR SHADOWS BEFORE	8
VII. WHERE DO WE GO FROM HERE?	9
VIII. THE SHAPE OF THINGS TO COME	9

Part II

THE DECISION AND ALTERNATIVES OPEN TO NORTH CAROLINA—A LEGAL ANALYSIS

I. THE DECISION	12
II. PRESERVING SEGREGATION BY PROVIDING FOR FREE EDUCATION IN PRIVATE SCHOOLS	12
1. The Proposal That the State Create a System of State-Supported Free Private Schools	12
2. The Proposal That the State Simply Pay Each Family with a School-Aged Child a Grant of Money to Secure His Education in Any Available Private School	15
III. THE PUBLIC SCHOOLS AND THE NEXT DECISION	17
1. The Time Element	17
2. The Element of Discretion	18
3. Geographical Variations in Approach and in Timing among Different Localities within the State	18
4. Taking Account of the Intensity of Racial Feeling	18
5. Taking Account of Differences in Academic Backgrounds between Negro and White Students	19
6. Taking Account of the Need to Protect the Health of Individual Students	19
7. Taking Account of the Personality, Needs and Desires of Individual Children	19
8. Summary and Comment	20
IV. POSSIBLE WAYS OF WORKING A "GRADUAL ADJUSTMENT"	20
1. Assignment	20
2. Redistricting	21
3. School Election	22
4. A System of Administrative Appeals	23
5. Institutions of Higher Learning	23
6. Treatment of Integrated Students	24
7. Revision of Existing Law	24
V. SUMMARY AND COMMENT	24

Part III

THE TEXT OF THE COURT'S DECISIONS

Cover Picture — The United States Supreme Court Building

POPULAR GOVERNMENT is published monthly except January, July, and August by the Institute of Government, The University of North Carolina, Chapel Hill. Editor: Albert Coates. Assistant Editors: Vernon Lee Bounds, William M. Cochrane, George H. Esser, Jr., Robert Edward Giles, Philip P. Green, Jr., Donald B. Hayman, Paul A. Johnston, Hurshell H. Keener, Edward Lane-Reticker, Henry W. Lewis, Roddey M. Ligon, Jr., John Alexander McMahon, Richard A. Myren, James C. N. Paul, Basil L. Sherrill. Editorial, business and advertising address: Box 990, Chapel Hill, N. C. Subscription: Per Year, $3.00; single copy, 35 cents. Advertising rates furnished on request. Entered as second class matter at the Post Office in Chapel Hill, N. C. The material printed herein may be quoted provided proper credit is given to POPULAR GOVERNMENT.

A Report to the Governor of North Carolina

On the Decision of the Supreme Court of the United States
on the 17th of May, 1954

Part I. The Background of the Decision

I
Letter of Transmittal

To His Excellency,
WILLIAM B. UMSTEAD,
Governor of North Carolina:

In compliance with your request we submit to you this study of legal problems growing out of the decision of the Supreme Court of the United States on the 17th of May, 1954. Part I outlines the background from which North Carolina looks at this decision. Part II discusses advantages and disadvantages of possible alternatives open to North Carolina within the framework of that decision. Part III gives the text of the Court's decision.

This study is submitted with the humility of those who know that great issues are at stake on which they would throw light without heat; that hopes and dreams and policies in many states are pinned on the validity of one proposal or another; that no one can speak with authority on any one of these proposals except the Court, and until the Court speaks no one can be sure of their acceptance or rejection; that the most we can do in this study is to lay bare the issues involved, point out the directions in which judicial winds appear to be blowing, and leave it to responsible officials of this State to choose and follow a given course of action.

It is beyond the scope and purpose of this study to urge the acceptance or rejection of any particular alternatives. It is beyond the scope and purpose of this study to urge the acceptance or rejection of the Supreme Court's invitation to give advice and counsel in formulating its decrees. It is within the scope and purpose of this study to outline legal issues involved in these alternatives with arguments advanced for and against them, together with considerations that might be urged upon the Court if its invitation for assistance is accepted.

It appears that at least three

By
Albert Coates
Director
Institute
of
Government

courses of action are open to North Carolina:

It can take the course that the Supreme Court has made its decision—let it enforce it; and meet the Court's efforts to enforce it with attitudes ranging from passive resistance to open defiance.

It can take the course that the Supreme Court of the United States has laid down the law, accept it without question, and proceed to mixed schools without delay.

It can take the course of seeking time in which to study plans of action, making haste slowly enough to avoid the provocative litigation and strife which might be a consequence of defying the decision, avoid the possibility of friction and strife which might be a consequence of precipitate acquiescence, and yet make haste fast enough to come within the law and keep the schools and keep the peace. We submit this study with the hope that it will be read in the spirit suggested by Sir Francis Bacon in his essay *Of Studies*: "Read not to contradict and confute; nor to believe and take for granted; nor to find talk and discourse; but to weigh and consider."

Respectfully submitted,
ALBERT COATES, *Director*
Institute of Government

II
The Negro Comes to North Carolina

Negroes came to North Carolina in 1526 as slaves with Spanish settlers in the Cape Fear region. They came with settlers from Virginia into the Albemarle region during the 1650's. In the Concessions of 1665 the Lords Proprietors of the Province of Carolina encouraged slavery by offering fifty acres of land to any settler bringing a Negro slave "above the age of fourteen years."

Around 800 Negroes were living in North Carolina by 1700; 15,000 by 1750; 140,000 by 1800; 361,000 by 1860; 624,000 by 1900; 1,000,000 by 1950.

Negroes were 30 per cent of the population by 1775; 29 per cent by 1800; 36 per cent by 1860; 38 per cent by 1880; 33 per cent by 1900; 25 per cent by 1950. Thus the Negro percentage has decreased slowly but steadily for the past seventy years. Around 361,000 of North Carolina's Negroes, or 34 per cent, live in urban areas with a high degree of segregation, and 685,000, or 66 per cent, live in rural areas with a low degree of segregation.

The Negro population varies by counties in North Carolina—from ten in Graham County to forty-nine thousand in Mecklenburg; from less than 1/5th of 1 per cent of the population in Graham County to 63.9 per cent in Northampton, as indicated on the following map.

Nine counties have 50 to 63.9 per cent Negro population: Martin, 50.3; Edgecombe, 51.9; Gates, 52.5; Hoke, 55.7; Halifax, 56.5; Bertie, 59.7; Hertford, 59.9; Warren, 62.9; Northampton, 63.9.

Twenty counties have 40 to 50 per cent: Wilson, 40.4; Bladen, 40.9; Tyrrell, 41.3; Wayne, 42.1; Hyde, 42.2; Nash, 42.4; Lenoir, 43.1; Chowan, 43.4; Washington, 43.6; Scotland, 43.7; Jones, 45.3; Vance, 45.4; Franklin, 45.6; Pitt, 46.2; Green, 46.5; Granville, 46.6; Caswell, 47.5; Perquimans, 47.7; Pender, 48.2; Anson, 48.5.

Sixteen counties have 30 to 40 per cent: Richmond, 30.4; New Hanover, 31.3; Robeson, 31.5; Currituck, 31.8; Chatham, 32.0; Craven, 32.3; Columbus, 33.0; Durham, 33.2; Pamlico, 34.5; Sampson, 35.2; Person, 35.5; Brunswick, 36.5; Duplin, 36.9; Beau-

WHITE AND NEGRO POPULATION BY COUNTIES IN 1950

PERCENTAGE OF NEGRO POPULATION

0% - 10%

10% - 25%

25% - 50%

OVER 50%

W—WHITE
N—NEGRO

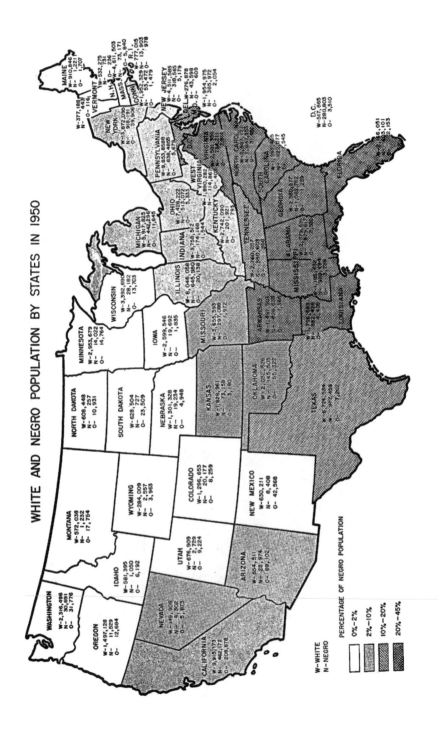

WHITE AND NEGRO POPULATION BY STATES IN 1950

PERCENTAGE OF NEGRO POPULATION

0%–2%
2%–10%
10%–20%
20%–45%

W–WHITE
N–NEGRO

fort, 37.3; Pasquotank, 38.0; Camden, 38.7.

Thirteen counties have 20 to 30 per cent: Rockingham, 20.0; Johnston, 21.7; Cleveland, 21.8; Union, 22.5; Montgomery, 22.9; Orange, 24.9; Mecklenburg, 25.3; Harnett, 25.4; Lee, 26.0; Moore, 26.8; Cumberland, 27.5; Forsyth, 28.3; Wake, 29.2.

Fifteen have 10 to 20 per cent: Davidson, 10.2; Stanly, 11.3; Buncombe, 12.2; Rutherford, 12.2; Carteret, 12.5; Lincoln, 12.6; Polk, 12.9; Gaston, 13.4; Davie, 13.9; Cabarrus, 15.2; Onslow, 15.7; Rowan, 17.0; Iredell, 17.7; Alamance, 18.4; Guilford, 19.5.

Eleven have 5 to 10 per cent: McDowell, 5.5; Surry, 5.7; Wilkes, 5.9; Henderson, 6.6; Caldwell, 6.9; Alexander, 7.0; Dare, 7.0; Burke, 7.4; Randolph, 8.4; Stokes, 8.9; Catawba, 9.0.

Sixteen have less than five per cent: Graham, 0.1; Mitchell, 0.3; Madison, 0.9; Clay, 1.1; Yancey, 1.1; Watauga, 1.2; Ashe, 1.2; Swain, 1.4; Avery, 1.5; Cherokee, 1.5; Jackson, 2.1; Macon, 2.1; Haywood, 2.1; Alleghany, 3.2; Transylvania, 4.9; Yadkin, 4.9.

Negroes in the United States. The fifteen million Negro population in the United States varies by states— from 257 in North Dakota to around 1,100,000 in Georgia; from 3/100ths of 1 per cent of the total population in North Dakota to 45 per cent in Mississippi.

Four and a half million Negroes are scattered over thirty-seven states, and ten and a half millions are concentrated in eleven southern states and the District of Columbia, as indicated on the following map.

Over four million Negroes in the northern and western states, or 93 per cent, live in urban areas with a high degree of segregation, and three hundred thousand, or 7 per cent, live in rural areas with a low degree of segregation.

The Negro population in the United States is grow ng in numbers and declining in percentage.

III

The Free Negro in North Carolina

From the early days in North Carolina some masters freed their slaves, and some slaves purchased their freedom. Five thousand free Negroes were listed in the census by 1790, fourteen thousand by 1820, thirty thousand by 1860. On January 1, 1863, President Lincoln's Emancipation Proclamation declared that "all slaves in rebellious states or parts of states should be then, thenceforward, and forever free." This proclamation did not free the slaves in any of the Union slave states, Tennessee, and certain portions of Virginia and Louisiana within Union military lines. Slaves in all states were freed in 1865 by the Thirteenth Amendment to the Constitution of the United States, providing that "Neither slavery nor involuntary servitude, except as a punishment for crime whereof the party shall have been duly convicted, shall exist within the United States, or any place subject to their jurisdiction."

Gradual Abolition of Slavery in Other States. In the *Quock Walker* case in 1781, the Supreme Court of Massachusetts held that the provision in its Bill of Rights that ". . . all men are born free and equal . . . ." freed the slaves, and no slaves are listed in Massachusetts in the census of 1790.

In 1780, Pennsylvania provided for gradual abolition of slavery by freeing the children born of slave mothers, giving them the rights of indentured servants but requiring them to serve their mothers' owners until they reached the age of twenty-eight. This general pattern of gradual abolition was followed by Vermont, Rhode Island, Connecticut, New Jersey, New York, and other states. Slavery was abolished in different states by different methods: legislative enactment, judicial decision, presidential proclamation, constitutional amendments, and the sheer force of public opinion. This process of gradual abolition extended for eighty-eight years —from 1777 to ratification of the Thirteenth Amendment in December, 1865.

IV

Schooling from 1665 to 1865

For White Children. Private schooling for white children in North Carolina had its beginnings in the teaching of missionaries and traveling preachers sent from England by the Society for the Propagation of the Gospel in Foreign Parts, together with scattered schools and academies growing up around outstanding teachers.

Public schooling for white children in North Carolina had its beginnings in acts of the General Assembly: in 1694, authorizing county courts to bind out destitute white orphan boys and girls as apprentices, with the requirement that their masters teach them to read and write; in 1764, authorizing the "Society for Promoting a Public School in New Bern," giving it state aid to pay for the schooling of ten poor children annually and to supplement the salary of the teacher; in 1825, creating the Literary Fund for common schools with dividends arising from bank stock owned by the State, and miscellaneous revenues; in 1839, dividing the "counties of the State into school districts," and calling upon the people in each district to vote on a tax to yield one dollar for every two dollars furnished by the Literary Fund. By 1860, one or two-room schoolhouses in 3700 districts were accessible to most of the people.

For Negro Children. Private schooling for Negro children in North Carolina followed in belated fashion the pattern of schooling for white children. By the 1800's some of the masters were teaching the more apt of their slaves to read and write and figure. This teaching was furthered in Sunday Schools and churches by many religious denominations. It was cut down but not cut out by the law of 1830 making it a misdemeanor to teach a slave to read and write. None of the public schools started under the law of 1839 was open to Negroes—slave or free.

In 1865, a meeting of Negro leaders in Raleigh petitioned the Constitutional Convention "for education for our children, that they may be made useful in all the relations of life." In 1866, the General Assembly required the masters of Negro orphan apprentices to teach them to read and write. Private schools for Negroes followed in the wake of the Union armies: by 1869, two hundred twenty-four teachers representing northern religious and benevolent societies were teaching eleven thousand Negro children in one hundred fifty schools, and four hundred or more teachers representing the Freedman's Bureau were teaching twenty thousand Negro children in more than four hundred schools. Tax supported schools for Negro children were around the corner, but they were not in sight.

The Problem of 1865. Before the meeting of the General Assembly the newly elected Governor of North Carolina wrote to a friend and adviser:

I am greatly at a loss on some of the graver matters which I shall be expected to discuss in my message and shall be much obliged to you for any suggestions from you on these or other matters. First—the negro question . . . I have no confidence that the condition of our negroes will be elevated by emancipation—but in our present condition I fear we shall have a Freedman's Bureau and military rule over us, if we make discrimination—as admittance in Common Schools. I mean if we educate the negroes in like manner—and your school fund being reduced to nothing and our people impoverished, I think the Common School system had better be discouraged, for a time, and thus avoid the question as to educating negroes . . . or shall I pass over this whole negro matter, putting it on the ground that an able commission having it in charge, by order of the General Assembly and Convention, it would be obtrusive for me to present my views.

In his message to the General Assembly the Governor stated: "Whatever may be our pecuniary distresses, our youth must be educated. We must sustain our institutions of learning."

Public Schools Abandoned in 1866. But the following session of the General Assembly in 1866: (1) abolished the offices of "Superintendent of Common Schools for the State" and "Treasurer of the Literary Fund," (2) took away state aid, (3) made the levy of local taxes for common schools discretionary with county officials, (4) authorized county officials to apply any taxes they might decide to levy to the aid of subscription schools, (5) authorized local school committees to allow subscription schools to be taught in the common schoolhouses by teachers qualified to teach in the common schools. Thus the General Assembly closed the doors of the common schools which had survived the stresses and strains of civil war to become the victim of poverty and the fear of mixed schools for white and Negro children.

University of North Carolina Abandoned in 1871. The University of North Carolina was conceived in the Constitution of 1776, chartered by the General Assembly of 1789, opened its doors in 1795, grew to four hundred fifty students by 1860, dwindled to a handful in 1865, closed its doors in the aftermath of civil war and the toils of reconstruction in 1871 to become the victim of poverty and political manipulation.

V

Schooling from 1865 to 1954

A. Separate Schools in North Carolina

The fear of mixed schools for white and Negro children which stifled public education in 1866 found expression again on the floor of the Constitutional Convention of 1868. The Committee on Education brought in a provision for a "general and uniform system of public schools." A clarifying amendment was offered providing for "separate and distinct schools" for white and Negro children. This amendment was voted down, but the substance of its meaning was incorporated in a resolution proclaiming to the State that "the interests and happiness of the two races would be best promoted by the establishment of separate schools."

A Negro representative in the Convention who had lived in Pennsylvania argued at length for separate schools:

In the state of Pennsylvania there is no law to my knowledge, certainly nothing in the organic law which prevents any man from sending his children to any school in his district, and yet there is no town in that state where there is any considerable number of colored children in which there are not separate schools. . . .

There will undoubtedly be separate schools in this State wherever it is possible, because both parties will demand it. My experience has been that the colored people in this State generally prefer colored preachers, when other things are equal, and I think the same will be found to be true respecting teachers. As the whites are in the majority in this State, the only way we can hope to have colored teachers is to have separate schools. . . .

The fear of mixed schools was confirmed in the Governor's plea for public schools in his inaugural address in 1868:

It is believed to be better for both [races], and most satisfactory to both, that the schools for the two, thus separate and apart, should enjoy equally the fostering care of the State. . . .

It is written in the records that the first public schools for white children started in 1839; that the General Assembly closed these schools to avoid opening them to Negro children in 1866; that all parties and factions insisted on separate schools in the Convention of 1868; that the General Assembly did not start writing a school law for white and Negro children in 1869 until a vote of 91 to 2 gave the assurance of separate schools; that an overwhelming vote in the Convention of 1875 made that assurance doubly sure by writing it into the framework of the Constitution; that the movement for public

education in the early 1900's was based upon it; that hundreds of millions of dollars have gone into the building of our statewide school system relying on the theory of separated schools, and many equalizing millions more have been planned upon that basis.

B. Separate Schools in Other States

The policy of separate schools for white and Negro children had been followed in many states and found expression in a succession of court decisions beginning in 1849.

In 1849, in *Roberts v. City of Boston* it was argued before the Massachusetts Supreme Court: (1) that a local ordinance providing for separate education of the races violated the provision in the Massachusetts Bill of Rights that all citizens are born equal; (2) that the operation of separate schools "tends to deepen and to perpetuate the odious distinction of caste, founded in a deep-rooted prejudice in public opinion." Chief Justice Shaw handed down the opinion of the court saying: (1) that segregation of the races did not in itself constitute discrimination; (2) that the Boston School Committee was acting within its powers when it provided substantially equal schools for Negroes; and (3) that any caste distinction aggravated by segregated schools "is not created by law and probably cannot be changed by law."

Pursuant to this decision segregated schools were upheld in Ohio in 1871, California and Indiana in 1874, in New York in 1883, and in Missouri in 1890.

In 1896, these precedents met with the approval of the United States Supreme Court in the case of *Plessy v. Ferguson*, where a Negro plaintiff sought to overthrow a Louisiana statute requiring separation of the races traveling on trains within the State as a violation of his personal rights guaranteed by the Thirteenth and Fourteenth Amendments. The Court denied his claim, saying:

Laws permitting, and even requiring [separation of the races] in places where they are liable to be brought in contact do not necessarily imply the inferiority of either race to the other and have been generally, if not universally, recognized as within the competency of the state legislatures in the exercise of their police power. The most common instance of this is connected with the establishment of separate schools for white and colored children which has been held a valid exercise of the legislative power, even by the courts of states where the political rights of the colored race have been longest and most earnestly enforced.

To this decision Justice Harlan filed a lone dissent:

> Our Constitution is color-blind, and neither knows nor tolerates classes among citizens. In respect of civil rights, all citizens are equal before the law. The humblest is the peer of the most powerful. The law regards man as man, and takes no account of his surroundings or of his color when his civil rights as guaranteed by the supreme law of the land are involved. It is, therefore, to be regretted that this high tribunal, the final expositor of the fundamental law of the land, has reached the conclusion that it is competent for a State to regulate the enjoyment by citizens of their civil rights solely upon the basis of race.

According to the Ashmore study of *The Negro and the Schools*, published in 1954, recent years have witnessed a decided trend to non-segregated schools in many sections of the country outside the South: "Many communities which have long maintained separate schools have moved away from segregation voluntarily, and for a variety of immediate reasons."

Only four states of the non-South now leave it to local school authorities to determine whether or not school children shall be separated by race. Arizona required segregation at the grade school level until 1951, when the law was amended to make it optional. Kansas permits segregation in the elementary schools of its largest cities and in the high school of only one—Kansas City. New Mexico allows the separation of white and Negro pupils, and Wyoming authorizes segregated facilities where there are fifteen or more Negro pupils. (There is no indication, however, that any Wyoming communities are exercising their option to segregate.) . . . . Of the remaining non-Southern states, eleven have no explicit legal provisions regarding segregation, while sixteen have laws specifically prohibiting it. Since the end of World War II three of the latter have moved affirmatively to end educational segregation within their borders. New Jersey included a strong anti-segregation provision in the new constitution adopted in 1947 and special legislation was passed to implement it; Indiana repealed its permissive segregation law in 1949 and substituted for it a statute outlawing racial distinctions in the public schools; Illinois, which had long required non-segregated education, strengthened the old law in 1949 by adding an effective penalty provision. The most important sanction—now employed by Illinois and New Jersey — is the withholding of state financial aid from any school district which maintains separate schools.

C. Progress of Schools in North Carolina
Under "Separate but Equal" Doctrine

Fear of Unequal Schools. The fear that "separate" schools for white and Negro children in North Carolina would not mean "equal" schools was expressed on the floor of the convention in 1868 in a proposal that "as ample, sufficient, and complete facilities be afforded for the one class as for the others . . . and . . . where the schools are divided the opportunity to each shall be equal."

It was expressed in argument by a Negro representative in the convention who opposed putting the requirement of segregation in the constitution, but favored separate schools by mutual consent:

> Make this distinction in your organic law and in many places the white children will have good schools at the expense of the whole people, while the colored people will have none or but little better than none.

It dangled over the heads of the people in a query from the State Superintendent of Public Instruction to the Attorney General of North Carolina on February 5, 1870: "If there is no adequate provision for their separate accommodation in the public schools of the township in which they reside, can colored children of lawful age be excluded from attending and receiving instruction in any free school that may be in operation?" There is no record of an answer.

The Fight for Schools. In 1866 white leaders advised the Negroes "first to find homes and work for themselves and then to provide education for their children." The notion that Negroes wanting an education would have to pay for their own schools freely expressed in 1866 was just as freely rejected in the public school law of 1869, providing for a "general and uniform system of public schools for both races" supported by taxation of the wealth of all the people for the children of all the people. The State moved in this direction, but not without protest, to the turn of the century.

A new force in public education appeared in North Carolina around the turn of the century and found expression in the leadership of Charles B. Aycock as he spoke to people thronging to hear him in all sections of the State—"If you vote for me [for Governor], I want you to do so with the distinct understanding that I shall devote the four years of my official term to the upbuilding of the public schools of North Carolina." He "pledged the State, its strength, its heart, its wealth, to universal education." He called school leaders together at the beginning of his administration and organized a "war upon illiteracy." He urged "the preachers, the teachers, the newspapers, and the mothers of North Carolina to be unceasing in their efforts to arouse the indifferent and compel by the force of public opinion the attendance of every child upon the schools."

Beneficiaries of the Fight. Negro children along with white children were beneficiaries of this fight for public schools. When a movement to restrict the Negro's opportunity for schooling by limiting Negro schools to Negro taxes started as he went into office, Governor Aycock told members of the General Assembly that "he would regard enactment of such legislation as a violation of his pledge to the people and of the plighted faith of his party, and if it were enacted he would resign his office and retire to private life."

When a similar movement gathered strength toward the end of his term of office he threw his weight against it in a formal message to the General Assembly which struck it down so decisively that it never again became a serious issue:

> It appears that both parties represented in your Honorable Body are pledged to at least a four months' school in every school district in the State and this, of course, includes the Negro districts. . . . It must be manifest that such a provision as this [segregating taxes] is an injustice to the Negro and injurious to us. No reason can be given for dividing the school fund according to the proportion paid by each race which would not equally apply to a division of the taxes paid by each race on every other subject. . . .
> The amendment proposed is unjust, unwise, and would wrong both races. . . . This would be a leadership that would bring us no honor and much shame. . . . Let us be done with this question, for while we discuss it the white children of the State are growing up in ignorance.

Governor Aycock's fight for Negro schooling is illustrated in the following utterances while he was in office: "I would not have the white people forget their duty to the negro. . . . We must not only educate ourselves but see to it that the negro has an opportunity for education. . . . Universal education means educating white and black alike. . . . If I had the power and the wealth to put a public schoolhouse in every district in North Carolina, I would enter into a guarantee that no child, white or black, in ten years from now should reach the age of twelve without being able to read and write. . . . As a white man I am afraid of but one thing for my race and that is that we shall become afraid to give the negro a fair chance. . . . The white man in the south can never attain to his fullest growth until he does absolute justice to the negro race. · · · My own opinion is that so far as we have done well, and that the future holds no menace for us if we do the duty which lies next to us, training, developing the coming generation, so that the problems which seem difficult to us shall be easy to them."

In the closing days of his administration he could say: "I have everywhere maintained the duty of the State to educate the negro. I have proclaimed this doctrine in many places and in doing so I have met the condemnation of friends whose good opinion I esteem; but holding my views, I could not have been worthy of the confidence of the great people of this State if I had remained silent. . . . The danger which I have apprehended is not that we shall do too much for the negro, but that becoming unmindful of our duty to him we shall do too little. · · · Let us cast away our fear of rivalry with the negro, all apprehension that he shall ever overtake us in the race of life. . . . Bid the negro Godspeed and at the same time put forward all the marvelous powers that are locked up in the big brain and throbbing heart of our own race."

D. Actions Speak Louder Than Words

With the fear of mixed schools removed, state and local units in North Carolina started forward in 1869 with a slowly but steadily expanding program of public education for white and Negro children.

School Population and Enrollment. 27,000 out of a white school-age population of 243,000 were enrolled in schools in 1870; 278,000 out of 439,000 in 1900; 606,000 out of 716,000 in 1930; 652,000 out of 792,000 in 1953. 13,000 out of a Negro school-age population of 141,000 were enrolled in schools in 1870; 131,000 out of 220,000 in 1900; 259,000 out of 315,000 in 1930; 276,000 out of 339,000 in 1953. Today, with white people making 74.3 per cent of the total

population in North Carolina, white children furnish 70.3 per cent of the enrollment in the public schools; and with Negroes making 25.7 per cent of the total population, Negro children furnish 29.7 per cent.

Length of Term. The average length of school term for white children was 50 days in 1880, 82 days in 1900, 148 days in 1925, 180 days in 1954. The average length of school term for Negro children was 49 days in 1880, 77 days in 1900, 136 days in 1925, 180 days in 1954.

Number of Teachers. There were 1100 white teachers in the public schools in 1870, 5000 in 1900, 16,000 in 1925, 20,000 in 1952. There were 490 Negro teachers in the public schools in 1870, 2500 in 1900, 5000 in 1925, 8000 in 1952. With 74.3 per cent of the population white in 1950, white teachers furnished 72.5 per cent of the teachers in the public schools; and with 25.7 per cent of the population Negro, Negro teachers furnished 27.5 per cent.

Teacher Load. The average teacher load for white teachers based on enrollment was 25 in 1820, 48 in 1900, 32 in 1925, 30 in 1952. The average teacher load for Negro teachers based on enrollment was 28 in 1870, 51 in 1900, 46 in 1925, 34 in 1952. Based on attendance the white teacher load in 1952 was 27.2 and the Negro teacher load was 29.5.

Salary of Teachers. The average annual salary for white teachers was $148.22 by 1905; $835.11 by 1925; $957.31 by 1940; $2,807.74 by 1952. The average annual salary of Negro teachers was $105.10 in 1905; $455.41 by 1925; $710.64 by 1940; $2,910.26 by 1952. The average salary of the white teacher increased over 300 per cent from 1925 to 1952; the average salary of the Negro teacher increased over 600 per cent. The Negro teacher salary caught up with the white teacher salary and passed it in 1945 and has kept the lead.

Value of School Property. White school property was valued at $1,335,250 by 1900; $21,670,514 by 1920; $103,724,982 by 1940; $316,487,762 by 1953. Negro school property was valued at $360,000 by 1900; $2,387,324 by 1920; $15,154,894 by 1940; $77,408,825 by 1953. In 1953 with 29.6 per cent of the total school enrollment, Negro school property was 19.6 per cent of the total school property value.

Expenditures for Current Operations. $23,829,740 was spent for current operation of white schools by 1929; $25,528,248 by 1940; $101,757,

966 by 1952. $4,086,792 was spent for current operation of Negro schools by 1929; $6,516,116 by 1940; $36,984,592 in 1952. With around 30 per cent of the total school enrollment, 14.6 per cent of the total funds for current operations went for Negro schools by 1929; 20.3 per cent by 1940; 26.7 per cent by 1952.

Literacy and Schooling. Eleven per cent of the Negroes over twenty years of age could read and write in 1870, forty-three per cent in 1900, seventy-three per cent in 1930, eighty-nine per cent in 1940, ninety-three per cent in 1950.

35,000 Negroes twenty-five years of age and over had no schooling by 1950; 50,000 had finished the first and second grades; 100,000 the third and fourth grades; 101,000 the fifth and sixth grades; 57,000 the seventh grade; 34,000 the eighth grade; 19,000 the ninth grade; 14,000 the tenth grade; 12,000 the eleventh grade; 16,000 the twelfth grade.

3000 had finished one year of college; 4000, two years of college; 2200, three years of college; 12,000, four years or more of college.

Apportionment of Bond Issue. A $50,000,000 appropriation and bond issue for public school buildings was authorized by the General Assembly and approved by the voters in 1949. With 30.2 per cent of the total school enrollment in 1949, 42 per cent of this capital outlay fund went for Negro schools. Another $50,000,000 bond issue, authorized and approved in 1953, is waiting on policy decisions for apportionment and distribution.

State Aid to Public Schools. In 1899 the State began supplementing local revenues for schools, to equalize facilities between poorer and richer counties, by amounts growing from $100,000 in 1900 to $6,000,000 in 1931. By 1932 the pattern changed from local support with State supplement to State support with local supplement, by amounts growing to $26,000,000 by 1940, to $87,000,000 by 1950, to $121,000,000 by 1954.

Higher Institutions of Learning. The General Assembly reopened the University in 1875, and created North Carolina State College of Agriculture and Engineering and Western Carolina College in 1889, Woman's College in Greensboro in 1891, Appalachian State Teachers College in 1903, and East Carolina College in 1907.

Resolutions offered in a meeting of the University Board of Trustees in 1868 suggested the creation of a department of the University for Negro students in some place "other than at Chapel Hill," and that "ample provision shall be made for affording the benefit of University education to colored pupils . . . which shall be equal in all respects to that furnished to white pupils at Chapel Hill." A committee recommended such a department, under the supervision of the State Superintendent of Public Instruction, with "authority to require the services of the professors of the University whenever this would not interfere with their duties at Chapel Hill."

No action was taken on this proposal; but in 1877 the General Assembly started providing 'higher education for Negroes—at Fayetteville State Teachers College in 1877, Agricultural and Technical College in Greensboro in 1891, Winston-Salem Teachers College in 1892, Elizabeth City State Teachers College in 1893, and North Carolina College in Durham in 1910.

Out of the Depths. This record of progress in education under separate school traditions must be read against the background of the years from 1865 to 1954. The Emancipation Proclamation followed by the Thirteenth Amendment destroyed an investment of $250,000,000 in slave property in North Carolina. Many sections of the State had been ravaged by occupying troops and foraging armies. Repudiation of all debts incurred in the prosecution of the war destroyed tens of millions of dollars of invested capital, closed every bank in the State, and wiped out countless private investors. The State Literary Fund which had been the financial backbone of the public school system since 1839 lost over 80 per cent of its capital invested in banks and railroads. In the words of a distinguished historian: "North Carolina entered upon the period with her public assets dissipated, her industries destroyed, her railroads wrecked, her educational institutions closed, her public debt piled up to crushing proportions, and with a political problem that for two generations absorbed those energies that should have been left free to develop the economic, social and intellectual resources of the State."

If from the vantage point of 1954 we look back to 1869 the record shows we have come a long way. If we look forward to the goal to which we have been moving we have a long way to go. But throughout this tradition of separate schools from 1869 to 1954 the record shows a steady improvement in school facilities for white and

Negro children. It shows a gradual, equalizing process underway, giving form and substance to the philosophy accepted by the State under the leadership of Aycock at the turn of the century: "Equal: That is the word. On that word I plant myself and my party—the equal right of every child born on earth to 'have the opportunity to bourgeon out all that there is within him."

VI

Coming Events Cast Their Shadows Before

"Separate but Equal" Doctrine Invoked to Compel Equality in 1935. The equalizing process underway in North Carolina was speeded in the 1930's and 40's by lawsuits in the federal courts invoking the "separate but equal" doctrine of *Plessy v. Ferguson* to compel equality of facilities in a series of cases accepting the principle and prescribing the methods of enforcement—in the *Murray* case from Maryland, the *Gaines* case from Missouri, the *Sipuel* case from Oklahoma, and the *McLaurin* case from Oklahoma.

The lawyers for the Negro plaintiffs argued and the courts held: that a lick and a promise in the direction of equality was not compliance with the *Plessy* doctrine; that equal schools in law meant equal schools in fact; that tuition scholarships to schools in other states did not constitute equality of opportunity; that to make assurance of equality doubly sure, Negroes would be admitted to white schools unless and until the Negro schools were equal to the white; that once admitted to white schools a Negro could not be segregated in library, classroom, or dining hall, and thus "impair and inhibit his ability to study, to engage in discussions and exchange views with other students and, in general, to learn his profession—appellant having been admitted to a state-supported school must receive the same treatment at the hands of the state as students of other races."

The Court said in the *Gaines* case, *supra*:

The basic consideration is not as to what sort of opportunities other states provide or whether they are as good as those in Missouri, but as to what opportunities Missouri itself furnishes to white students and denies to Negroes solely upon the ground of color. . . . Here petitioner's right was a personal one. It was as an individual that he was entitled

to the equal protection of the laws, and the state was bound to furnish him within its borders facilities for legal education substantially equal to those which the state has afforded for persons of the white race. . . .

In April 1951, following a decision of the U. S. Court of Appeals for the Fourth Circuit, the Board of Trustees of the Consolidated University of North Carolina passed the following resolution:

In all cases of applications for admission by members of racial groups, other than the white race, to the professional or graduate schools when such schools are not provided by and in the State of North Carolina for such racial groups, the application shall be processed without regard to color or race, as required by authoritative judicial interpretation of the Constitution of the United States, which is the supreme law of our state as well as of the nation, and the applicant accepted or rejected in accordance with the approved rules and standards of admission for the particular school.

Since June 1951, ten Negroes have been admitted to the University law school. Two have been admitted to the summer sessions of the graduate school. Two have been admitted to the medical school. Two have been admitted to the graduate division of State College engineering school.

The Ground of Argument Shifts in 1950. In 1950, the argument shifted to the point of view that even if facilities were equal, segregation was in itself an inequality, a denial of equal protection of the laws, and a discrimination against the Negro, violating the Fourteenth Amendment. The United States Supreme Court did not decide this question in the *Sweatt* case from Texas but noted it in these words:

What is more important, the University of Texas Law School possesses to a far greater degree those qualities which are incapable of objective measurement but which make for greatness in a law school. Such qualities, to name but a few, include reputation of the faculty, experience of the administration, position and influence of the alumni, standing in the community, traditions and prestige.

Two years later in *Brown v. Board of Education* the lawyers for Negro plaintiffs attacking the segregation of white and Negro students in the schools of Topeka, Kansas admitted that the separate schools were substantially equal and pressed the argument advanced in the *Sweatt* case, *supra.*

The 17th of May, 1954. This argument was accepted by the Supreme Court of the United States in a unanimous decision written by the Chief Justice and handed down on the 17th of May, 1954, in these words:

> We conclude that in the field of public education the doctrine of "separate but equal" has no place. Separate educational facilities are inherently unequal. Therefore, we hold that the plaintiffs and others similarly situated for whom the actions have been brought are, by reason of the segregation complained of, deprived of the equal protection of the laws guaranteed by the Fourteenth Amendment.

Coming events had long been casting their shadows before. The spectre of a cloud the size of a man's hand in Justice Harlan's dissent on the far-off horizon of 1896 had been growing in the sky with court decisions handed down in quick succession since the *Murray* case in 1935. But all of these successive warnings in the swiftly cumulating cloud did not prepare the rank and file of people in North Carolina for the flash of lightning on the 17th of May. Many people have been a little blinded by the light, and are groping for an answer to the question—Where do we go from here?

VII

Where Do We Go from Here?

The past is history and the future is mystery.

It is idle to speculate on whether the General Assembly of North Carolina would have ratified the Fourteenth Amendment to the Constitution of the United States, if members had thought it would then or later prohibit separate schools for white and Negro children; or on whether or when the General Assembly would have reopened the public schools if it had thought the Fourteenth Amendment would then or later prohibit separate schools.

It is idle to speculate on what would have happened to the public schools in 1896 if the Supreme Court of the United States had followed the dissenting opinion of Justice Harlan in *Plessy v. Ferguson* that the Fourteenth Amendment was color-blind and prohibited separate schools even if they were equal.

It is idle to speculate on the difference in the future of the public schools for the next generation if the Supreme Court of the United States had not removed the compelling motive for bringing Negro schools up to the level of white schools in order

to keep Negro children out of white schools, or whether equality in white and Negro schools for the last fifty years would have forestalled or delayed the Court's decision.

The Problem of Keeping the Peace. It is *not* idle to speculate on the threat of unbridled passions to the public peace if the separate white and Negro school traditions bend into a focus under pressure of the Court's decision. People were not ready for mixed schools in 1866 and many raise the question as to what extent, if any, they are ready for them now. Possibilities are suggested running all the way from immediate integration of the schools to resisting the Court's decision regardless of the consequences.

Law and order is not a gift of the gods; it is an achievement of men and women which must be affirmed or lost in every generation. The people of North Carolina have achieved it through slow and painstaking struggle for 300 years—from the 1650's, when pioneering settlers, few and far between, started out into the wilderness as laws unto themselves, and slowly worked their way from isolated cabins, to scattered settlements, to a connected commonwealth in the framework of a federal union, with all the interlocking, overlapping, and conflicting relationships involved in the keeping of the peace. We have seen the mob, the riot, and the Ku Klux Klan in action often enough in our experience to know what happens when men take the law into their own hands and trample under foot the peace and dignity of the State.

The Problem of Keeping the Schools. It is *not* idle to speculate on the future of the public schools under pressure of the 17th of May decision. Public school doors closed in 1866. And though the poverty of 1866 has largely disappeared, racial feeling has not yet disappeared. Possibilities are suggested running all the way from integrating schools without delay to abandoning the public schools altogether.

The people of North Carolina have achieved their schools as they have achieved law and order—through slow and painful struggles: from the requirement in 1694 that an orphan apprentice should be taught by his master to read and write, to private schools for some white children in the 1700's, to public schools for all white children in 1839, to public schools for all white and Negro chil-

dren in 1869, to compulsory schooling for all white and Negro children in 1907. They moved from state aid to local schools in 1839, to state supplement with local support in 1899, to state support with local supplement in 1933. They moved from local district schools in the 1840's to county-wide school systems by the 1920's, to a statewide school system in the 1930's. These highlights of a hundred years of struggle may flicker and go out in gusts of fear or passion gone beyond control.

It is written in Article I, §29 of the Constitution of North Carolina that: "A frequent recurrence to fundamental principles is absolutely necessary to the preservation of liberty." This is wholesome gospel today as some people look on the Court's decision as destructive of the social order in which they have lived and moved and had their being, while other people look on it as another milestone in the long unbroken struggle of a race from slavery to freedom; as some give way to understandable jubilation over a hard-won victory, while others give way to understandable despair at judicial blighting of a long-cherished way of life.

For if extremists in the white and Negro races crush the moderating forces, or push the rank and file of the people out of the middle of the road into the ditch on either side, we shall find the answer to the question of what happens when an irresistible force hits an immovable object in an inconceivable catastrophe. If this inconceivable catastrophe is to be avoided, time must be given for moderation on both sides while extremists on each side are shouting that there is no other side.

VIII

The Shape of Things To Come

The Court's Decrees. In its 17th of May decision the Court went out of its way to grant permission to all states "requiring or permitting segregation" in the public schools to give advice and counsel in adapting its decrees to the "problems of considerable complexity" in a "great variety of local conditions."

This tacit invitation shifts the spotlight to southern and border state officials as they wrestle with a problem in the making for three hundred years, coming down to them unsolved from generation to generation with the haunting overtones of a mysterious torment, and pointed up by a decision creating as many problems as it solves.

The Governor of North Carolina and the Attorney General have accepted this opportunity on the theory that North Carolina has everything to gain and nothing to lose by filing a brief and participating in the hearing; that the decrees to be handed down by the Court will be binding as a precedent on every one of the seventeen states "requiring or permitting segregation," whether they appear or not; that participating in the hearing gives the last clear chance for the State to argue to the Court for flexible decrees which will give the people of North Carolina the greatest possible freedom of action in the operation of their schools.

They are proceeding on the theory that this tacit invitation of the Court is an open recognition of the problems these seventeen states are up against and of the difference in degree of Negro population which makes a difference in the kind of problem faced: (1) by states with one Negro, or five or ten, in a hundred persons, and states with twenty, thirty, or forty-five; (2) by counties within the borders of a state where the Negro population climbs to fifty or more in a hundred, or sixty-three in a hundred as in Northampton County, North Carolina, or to eighty-four in a hundred as in Macon County, Georgia; (3) by urban areas where residential patterns cut the mixed attendance problem down to size, and rural areas where residential patterns aggravate the problem.

They are going on the theory that differing intensities in racial feeling growing out of differing densities in Negro population may perhaps explain why some states never resorted to separate schools for white and Negro children, why border states are already proceeding with plans for integrating white and Negro schools, why southern states are waiting on the Court's decrees, why some state officials are slow to appear before the Court to argue even for gradual adjustment to the terms of a decision so many of their constituents are unwilling to accept at all, and why some of them feel driven to the desperation of defying the Court's decree.

They are giving advice and counsel on the theory that differences in degree of Negro population, making a difference in the kind of problem, may make a difference in the Court's decrees; that a Court which refuses to continue a policy it believes to be wrong will refuse to inaugurate a policy it believes to be right in a wrong way; that the Constitution of the United States can afford to take into consideration the constitution of human nature and allow for time with healing in its wings.

The Role of State and Local School Officials. Our leaders and ourselves may turn for light and learning on this question to state and local school officials who have been working with white and Negro principals, teachers, and children for years and have already acquired knowledge and experience that committees starting now could not accumulate in years. With this background, they can foresee the multiplicity of problems which will be involved if mixed school attendance is invoked—from the time children get on school busses in the morning, through classroom hours, school recesses, and student activities, till the end of the bus ride home in the afternoon.

Under the leadership of the State Superintendent of Public Instruction they can map every white and Negro residence in every local school district and city and county administrative unit in the State; locate and describe the school facilities used by white and Negro children; translate colorless statistics into problems of flesh and blood that they will face if separate schooling should be abandoned all at once or by the slow steps of gradual adjustment; and explore the possible vantage points from which gradual adjustment might start upon its course of trial and error—if the schools are to be preserved, and if they are to operate within the framework of the law.

Many local school boards and officials scattered through the State are already trying to fit the Court's decision to the ground in their respective units, in a spirit illustrated by the following resolution:

This board is confident of its ability and that of local citizens to face any problems which may be occasioned by this Supreme Court ruling with level headed realism and sobriety . . . and it is the intent and purpose of this board . . . to conduct a preliminary appraisal and analysis of this ruling to the end that when final decisions and policies are made, any necessary adjustment in the local school system may be effected with a minimum of difficulty and a maximum of patient understanding, vision, good will, and cooperation.

Realistic local studies such as these by local school boards and officials are needed now in every administrative unit in the State:

To give needed underpinning to the

Attorney General's brief and argument as he prepares the case for North Carolina;

To inform the discussions of the Governor's committee as it tackles the knottiest problem any State committee in our history ever faced;

To guide the deliberations of the Governor and the General Assembly as they come to grips with the most explosive question faced in any legislative session since 1865;

To help the rank and file of the people lift discussions of this problem out of the bogs of emotion and the sloughs of despond and root them in the solid ground of fact.

Historic Questions. The 17th of May decision, removing the compelling motive of maintaining a ninety-year tradition of separate schools, faces the people of North Carolina with hard and bitter questions. Will we continue lifting public school facilities in the future as in the past? Will we lift the poorer school facilities to the level of the better? lower the better to the level of the poorer? or lower both to an all time low?

Will well-to-do parents withdraw their children from the public schools and take on the added economic burden of sending them to private schools supported wholly by themselves, while leaving the public schools to the Negroes and the poorer white folks, thus aggravating the racial antagonisms which seem to hover along the economic border lines?

Will we do away with compulsory school attendance so as to give the poorer white folks the choice of sending their children to school with Negro children or growing up in ignorance?

Will we abandon public schooling altogether as we did in 1866, and lose ourselves in stultifying bitterness, while other states and sections go on to lift their schooling standards?

Abiding answers to these mysterious and tormenting questions, if found at all, will not be found in fighting phrases, or in stirring slogans, or defiant gestures. They will be found in the differing viewpoints and clashing opinions coming out of the mind and heart and conscience of our leaders and ourselves, colored with something of the gall and gorge of all of us, and tempered with the saving grace of a charity that suffereth long and is kind. They will be found in the meaning of a poet three thousand years ago as he wrote the "God whose law it is that he who learns must suffer . . . until against our will, and even in our own despite, comes wisdom to us by the awful grace of God."

A Time for Greatness. In the trials and errors of the days ahead we must not forget that we are the children of a people who in the 17th and 18th centuries had the vision and stamina to pull up their roots from European soil and start a new life in the American wilderness; who saw the things they gave their lives to broken in the 1860's and found resources in themselves to build the foundations of a new civilization out of the ruins of civil war and the bitterness of reconstruction; who in the years that followed let the dead past, in part at least, bury its dead, came to working adjustments with 360,000 slaves turned freedmen, found a way to open the doors of public schools to white and Negro children in local districts, and after 1900 began to build in equalizing measure the state-wide system of separated schools which is our pride today.

We are the heirs of great traditions in the schools of North Carolina—symbolized by Archibald Murphey in the early 1800's; Calvin Wiley in the 1850's and 60's; Aycock, Joyner, and McIver in the 1900's. Like a bell from distant hilltops we can hear their names today—ringing out to us the spirit of a people that sees in disaster only a challenge the brighter to burn, and which, when darkness hedges it about, builds in itself a dwelling place of light.

Let us pray that it is not too much to hope that the children of those people will bend all of their energies to find a way to save the solid values three generations have built into the schools; that we will find a way to avoid the losses which for the moment appear both frightful and inevitable to all too many people; that we will find a power in us greater than ourselves to dissolve corroding and disruptive issues as fast as they arise; for we cannot keep the schools if we do not keep the peace.

Let us pray that the gradual adjustment which was not allowed in the tragic years that followed 1865 may be allowed in the years that follow the 17th of May decision in 1954. The haunting memory of those tragic years summons the vision of a South that might have been to go with the spokesmen for North Carolina, as they plead with the Supreme Court of these not so sovereign but still united states not to move so fast it will postpone the coming of the South which men and women of differing colors, creeds, and races here in North Carolina must help to build in the light and shadow of the Court's decrees.

_____

The foregoing article is a shorter version of the original report. Citations, tables, and charts have been omitted.

THE GOVERNOR'S SPECIAL ADVISORY COMMITTEE ON EDUCATION

Dr. F. D. Bluford of Greensboro, President of the A. & T. College; J. H. Clark of Elizabethtown, former member of the State Senate and now Chairman of the North Carolina Medical Care Commission; Miss Ruth Current of Raleigh, formerly of Rowan County, now State Home Demonstration Agent; Dr. Gordon Gray of Chapel Hill, President of the University of North Carolina; Fred B. Helms of Charlotte, former President of the North Carolina State Bar Association, and now a member of the State Judicial Council; Dallas Herring of Rose Hill, Chairman of the Duplin County Board of Education; R. O. Huffman of Morganton, former President of The Business Foundation; W. T. Joyner of Raleigh, prominent lawyer and civic leader; Mrs. Helen S. Kafer of New Bern, Administrator of the Kafer Memorial Hospital, former President of the New Bern Parent-Teacher Council, and now a member of the New Bern City School Board; Holt McPherson of High Point, Editor of the High Point Enterprise; James C. Manning of Williamston, Superintendent of Schools in Martin County; Mrs. Hazel Parker of Tarboro, Home Demonstration Agent, Edgecombe County; Thomas J. Pearsall of Rocky Mount, farmer and businessman, former Speaker of the House of Representatives, and Chairman of this Committee; Dr. Clarence Poe of Raleigh, Chairman of the Board of Editors of the Progressive Farmer; I. E. Ready of Roanoke Rapids, Superintendent of Roanoke Rapids City Schools; Dr. Paul Reid of Cullowhee, President of Western Carolina College; Dr. J. W. Seabrook of Fayetteville, President of Fayetteville Teachers College; Judge L. R. Varser of Lumberton, formerly an Associate Justice of the Supreme Court of North Carolina, and now Chairman of the State Board of Law Examiners; Arthur D. Williams of Wilson, Chairman of the Wilson County Board of County Commissioners.

Part II. The Decision and Alternatives Open To North Carolina---A Legal Analysis

This article is a much-shortened version of the Institute's legal analysis of the Supreme Court's decision and of the alternatives open to North Carolina in light of that decision. This legal analysis was a part of the Institute's "Report to the Governor of North Carolina on the Decision of the United States Supreme Court on the 17th of May, 1954."

Most of the discussion which appeared in the original report has been condensed and some parts have been omitted entirely. In a few places the language of the original report has been rewritten in the interest of supplying a summary and more easily understandable statement of the legal issues. Legal citations have been excluded.

Readers desiring a more detailed discussion of the legal arguments treated in this article, with the citation of legal authority, are referred to the original report. This report is now being published by the Institute, and copies will be available to the general public upon request.

The Decision

Beginning in 1950 and spreading into 1952, five separate lawsuits were commenced. In Kansas, in South Carolina, in Virginia, in Delaware and in the District of Columbia hundreds of Negro parents and their children joined together to sue local school authorities.

These suits asked the courts to declare that enforced segregation of Negro school children from white children violated the federal constitution. The Fourteenth Amendment declares: "No state . . . shall deny to any person . . . the equal protection of the laws." Segregation, said these Negro plaintiffs, was not "equal protection;" hence it violated their constitutional rights.

The school boards and the states involved denied this claim; they argued that "separate but equal" schools were permissible under the constitution. They pointed to language in a case decided in 1896—*Plessy v. Ferguson*—which said just that, and they pointed out that the Supreme Court had never overruled this interpretation.

The Negro plaintiffs lost in the lower courts, although two of these courts, after hearing extensive evidence, found as a "fact" that segregation had a harmful effect on Negro students. As was expected, all of the plaintiffs carried their cases to the Supreme Court for review. Twice the Court heard extensive arguments from both sides dealing with the many grave questions relating to school segregation. On May 17, 1954, after long and deliberate consideration of the issues, the Court rendered the answer.

A unanimous opinion, styled Brown v. Topeka Board of Education, stated in part:

. . . Does segregation of children in public schools solely on the basis of race, even though the physical facilities and other

By
James C. N. Paul

Assistant Director Institute of Government

"tangible" factors may be equal, deprive the children of the minority group of equal educational opportunities? We believe that it does.

. . . To separate them from others of similar age and qualifications solely because of their race generates a feeling of inferiority as to their status in the community that may affect their hearts and minds in a way unlikely ever to be undone.

. . . We conclude that in the field of public education the doctrine of "separate but equal" has no place. Separate educational facilities are inherently unequal. Therefore, we hold that the plaintiffs and others similarly situated for whom the actions have been brought are, by reason of the segregation complained of, deprived of the equal protection of the laws guaranteed by the Fourteenth Amendment.

The decision (hereafter called the Brown decision) was prospective in its effect; it stated a proposition of constitutional law, but it deliberately failed to state how and when this proposition is to be enforced. The question of "how" and "when" was set down for further argument. All states that presently retain segregated schools may appear at this argument.

There can be no question but that North Carolina has been directly affected. The Brown decision eucompasses all schools, and it declares that laws requiring segregation of the races are no longer enforceable. Wrote Chief Justice Warren: "We have this day held that the Equal Protection Clause of the Fourteenth

Amendment prohibits the states from maintaining racially segregated schools."

But, for the present, the status quo remains. Were a Negro to sue today for admittance to a white school tomorrow, his suit would in all probability be held in abeyance. The Supreme Court has stayed its hand. No changes need be ordered until the Supreme Court first decides what must be done. And that—what must be done to comply—is an open question. There are yet many possibilities which may be less revolutionary than some reaction might lead one to suspect.

Preserving Segregation by Providing for Free Education In Private Schools

The Brown decision dealt with segregation in the public schools, but it did not deal with private schools. And it has been suggested that the State could yet preserve both free education and also segregation by providing for the creation of free private schools.

How can this be done? Basically there would seem to be two different approaches. First, the State could play an active role in the creation, financial support and supervision of the private schools. Second, the State could do nothing except provide grants to pay for the tuition of all children who qualify for admittance to a private school. We will discuss the legality of both plans.

1. The Proposal That the State Create a System of State-Supported Free Private Schools

Proposed statutes in other southern states, drawn to achieve this plan, authorize groups of private citizens to establish "private" educational institutions. State or local authorities are authorized to lease public school buildings and grounds at nominal rates to these private organizations which would run private schools. These private schools would be maintained by an allocation of state revenue, so that it would cost the student little or nothing to attend them. Under the proposed statutes, receipt of state funds for maintenance would subject the private schools to state supervision over curricula, textbooks, teachers' salaries and other teaching and instructional standards. By utilizing the grant of power to charter private schools, each community would be able to organize schools which could pursue any admission policy which the incorporators or the governing body of the school saw fit to pursue.

The theory of the free private school plan is this: The private schools would not be subject to the requirements of the Fourteenth Amendment. The Fourteenth Amendment applies only to the states. It says: *"No state"* can deny *"equal protection of the laws."* (Emphasis added.) It says nothing about private individuals or private corporations denying *"equal protection."* The Supreme Court has held that the exclusion of Negroes by privately owned institutions such as hotels and restaurants does not violate the constitution because these enterprises are not state activities; they involve no "state action," and the Fourteenth Amendment only applies to "state action."

But would state-supported free private schools involve "state action"? That is the critical question.

The Supreme Court has decided a number of recent cases dealing with the "state action" problem. All of these have dealt with alleged racial discriminations wrought by private persons having no official connection with the state. True, these cases lay down no single all-inclusive test which will enable the lawyer to predict in a moment whether the proposed private schools will be subject to the Fourteenth Amendment; the Court has had before it no case involving the exact question which we now seek to answer. Yet the recent precedents may supply important clues to the law.

In these recent cases, the Court has found "state action" by employing, apparently, one of three possible methods of analysis. In the "restrictive covenant cases," the Court approached the problem by seeking to determine how far the state had gone to exert sovereign power to help the private parties execute their purpose. In the so-

called "white primary" cases the Court was confronted with a situation where there was no active exertion of state power at all, and yet it found state activity by deciding that the private parties were discharging an important governmental function. In a third line of cases involving trade unions, the Court indicated that a private organization which receives special powers and privileges from the sovereign cannot use these advantages to work racial discriminations.

We consider then:
(1) The racial restrictive covenant cases,
(2) The primary election cases,
(3) The union cases,
and their bearing on the question of "state action."

The Racial Restrictive Covenant Cases. It has long been settled that any racial zoning ordinance which requires the separation of Negro and white residential areas—i.e., which prohibits members of one race from buying and occupying certain properties set aside exclusively for members of the other race—is a violation of the Fourteenth Amendment.

In 1948 and again in 1953, the Supreme Court was faced with this problem: If private persons make a private contract agreeing among themselves to exclude some racial group from the occupancy of certain land, can the state's courts enforce the agreement? If the courts help the parties enforce their "private" racial restrictive covenant, would this constitute "state action" in violation of the Fourteenth Amendment?

The Court determined that enforcement of the private exclusion was "state action." The Court noted that by enforcing the agreements the state allowed private persons to invoke the "coercive power" of the courts to secure compliance with the private racial restriction; thus, the state helped and encouraged private citizens to make and abide by these contracts; in short the state had an active hand in implementing a racial exclusion by private citizens. This use of power by the state amounted to "state action"; and because the state had actively helped others do what the state could not do by itself, this was "state action" in violation of the Fourteenth Amendment. Significantly, the Court said: "State action refers to *exertions of state power in all forms.* And when the effect of

that action is to deny rights subject to the protection of the Fourteenth Amendment, it is the obligation of this Court to enforce the constitutional commands." (Emphasis added.)

In the free private school plan now under consideration the state would exert power to help and encourage the operation of the private schools by providing special enabling legislation, by leasing real property to the schools, by supplying them with the financial wherewithal to operate, and by supervising teacher salaries and instructional standards.

This is not exactly the same exertion of sovereign power that was present in the covenant cases, but there are some parallels. In both situations it is the positive action of the state which makes possible the exclusion of Negroes by the private parties. This exertion of state power might subject the proposed free private schools to the limitations of the Fourteenth Amendment.

The Primary Election Cases. It has long been settled by a series of court decisions that no state and no political party can by law, or by action of its officials, prevent a person from voting in an official primary election solely because of his race. Such action violates both the Fourteenth and Fifteenth Amendments.

As a result of those decisions, the legislature of South Carolina repealed all laws relating to the management of primary elections. It was the State's manifest purpose to treat each political party as a private club, and to leave these clubs totally free to decide for themselves who could participate in their affairs.

Acting in this capacity, the Democratic Party then passed a rule which excluded Negroes from voting in its primary. When challenged in the courts, the party argued that it had become a purely private organization—like any other private club—because the State no longer regulated any of its affairs and provided no rules whatsoever to govern its primary elections.

The federal courts disagreed. The label "private club" which the government of South Carolina had affixed to the party was deemed irrelevant. The crucial fact was that the party conducted statewide elections to nominate candidates for public office. It was engaging in "an important function relating to the exercise of sovereignty;" it was exercising a power—regulating elections—

which governments traditionally exercise. And the Court declared: When the state allows a private organization to exercise such a power, then the private organization engages in "state action," and it is subject to the constitution's prohibitions against racial exclusion.

This principle, laid down in the South Carolina cases, was expressly recognized and followed by the Supreme Court in a recent case involving a private political organization in Texas.

Possibly these voting cases are inapplicable to our present problem ("state action" and free private schools) because they dealt with the right to cast a ballot and not school attendance. But again . there are parallels between the voting cases and the free private school problem. There exists at least a possibility that the Court might treat the running of state-supported, free private schools as the operation of a state activity for the same reason that it treated the management of a primary election as a state activity. The Court might carry the primary case reasoning over into the school field, because it might decide that the providing of a system of *free* education, like the managing of an election, is a vital and a traditional governmental function. According to the decision of the Court in the *Brown* case, the providing of free education has come to be "perhaps the most important function of state and local governments." Of course the Court's dictum was not necessarily meant to guide future "state action" decisions. It does not necessarily settle the private school issue. Still, the Court might approach the legality of proposed free private school laws with the assumption in mind that over the last century the states have given "recognition" to "the importance of education to our democratic society" as the very basis of "good citizenship." That is the way the Court described state-supported education in its *Brown* decision; hence the Court might assume that free private schools which received financial maintenance from the state would be an attempt to conduct public schools under private management.

The Union Cases. It has long been settled that a state cannot exclude a person from designated fields of employment solely because of his race or creed.

Within recent years cases have arisen involving the powers of trade unions to accomplish the same result

by bargaining openly with employers to secure the dismissal of workers of a particular race. In such cases the unions have argued that they were purely private organizations, that this conduct—admittedly "discriminatory"—was beyond the reach of law, for the discrimination, so it was argued, was the product of private and not governmental action.

The Court has regularly rejected these arguments. True, said the Court, a union is a private organization, but a union's status is not like that of just any private organization. Once it is certified by the government as the bargaining agent in an industry, the union is automatically invested by statute with certain extraordinary powers; it is given an exclusive authorization to deal with the employer—to contract for wages and fix other conditions of employment. In other words, the government makes it possible for the union to play a special and powerful role in the community of workers who make up the industry. Given such special powers, the union is bound to exercise them without achieving any illegal discriminations between employees.

Perhaps the union cases must be confined to the employment situation, or, in any event, perhaps there is no suitable analogy to the free private school problem. But again, there are certain parallels.

The Court of Appeals for the Fourth Circuit relied on the union cases when it decided that the opera-

tion of a privately operated school which was heavily supported by state funds and which denied admission to Negroes involved "state action" in violation of the Fourteenth Amendment. The specially created private school, like the certified union, is given unusual benefits and advantages by the state to fulfill an important function; the school like the union is treated differently by the sovereign—differently from other private groups; the school like the union depends upon these state-bestowed ad-

Seated, Governor William B. Umstead. Standing, left to right: Victor S. Bryant of Durham, Chairman of the Commission on Higher Education; Thomas J. Pearsall of Rocky Mount, Chairman of the Governor's Special Advisory Committee on Education; John A. Pritchett of Windsor, member of the State Board of Education and Chairman of the Board's Fact Finding Committee; The Honorable Luther Hodges of Leaksville, Lieutenant Governor of North Carolina and Chairman of the State Board of Education; Fred Folger of Mt. Airy, Chairman of the Commission on the Revision of the Public School Laws; Frank Taylor of Goldsboro, former Speaker of the House and Legislative Adviser to the Governor; and The Honorable Harry McMullan of Raleigh, Attorney General of North Carolina.

vantages to accomplish its mission. Perhaps, as the Court of Appeals declared, the state-sponsored private school, like the government-certified union, cannot legally use its special privileges to the disadvantage of one particular race; and perhaps this would mean that such a school could not offer benefits to some members of the community and deny them to others solely on the grounds of race.

Summary. It is readily apparent from the above that there is no square precedent or "rule of law" which settles the private school issue. The problem is one of deciding whether there is or is not "state action" in the operation of the school. And the cases have not tackled this issue by discussing the "state action" doctrine in broad abstract terms. Still, some generalizations may perhaps be offered. The cases show that labels mean little; simply calling a school "private" won't make it a private school; nor is it decisive that an alleged racial discrimination has been wrought by some person or group who are not official representatives of the state. No one Supreme Court precedent decides the issue, but it is apparent that the proposed free private school would partake of many of the very elements which led the Court to find "state action" in the activities of other private groups involved in the cases just discussed. This combination of factors might mean that the courts would hold that a free private school, organized along the lines discussed, could not deny admission to otherwise qualified Negroes who sought to attend them.

2. The Proposal That the State Simply Pay Each Family with a School-Aged Child a Grant of Money To Secure His Education in Any Available Private School

There are many variations to the private school plan. The plan just discussed involves extensive state participation in the operation of the schools. But the State might set up another type of private school system which would provide for much less state participation. Thus, at the opposite pole from the plan just discussed stands a suggestion that the State should simply advance a grant of money for educational purposes to the families of school-aged children who desire that their children no longer attend public schools.

For convenience sake this may be called the "tuition grant" plan. The proposal anticipates the growth of free private schools throughout the State. But the State would do nothing to help others create these free private schools; each community would be on its own; there would be no lease of public school property to private educational organizations at nominal rates. The private school would have to acquire its property and other facilities without any economic help from the State. All this would be done to attempt to provide a system of private schools that involved no "state action;" for otherwise, as noted, the private school might be required to permit mixed attendance just like the public schools. The only economic assistance extended by the State towards private education would be the payment of a lump sum of money to the parents of each school child who can attend a private school—with a stipulation that this tuition grant would only be spent to defray tuition to a private school.

This plan goes, perhaps, to the fullest possible extent to minimize the possibility of a finding of "state action." Of course, these extreme measures taken to forestall "state action" may make the plan undesirable or impracticable on its face. A multitude of problems may come to mind: assuming that one vital purpose of free schooling is to supply training for citizenship, could the State be sure that the private schools which it was supporting provided such training? In return for the "tuition grant," freely given to each parent, would the State have any guarantee that it could get anything like its money's worth out of the schooling provided in these private schools? Would the children be assured of adequate physical school facilities? Would the schools, operating without any close supervision by the State, meet appropriate academic standards so that children who attended them would be able to secure admittance to colleges and professional institutions? What would happen to the standards of education in this State? There will be no discussion here of these problems. They involve discussion of educational policy and sociological problems. This is a legal study. But there are some purely legal problems which must be reckoned with if this "tuition grant" plan were to be proposed.

The "Public Purpose" Problem. There is a doctrine of constitutional law which says that public funds must be spent for a "public purpose." This "public purpose" doctrine is rooted in both the Fourteenth Amendment and the Constitution of North Carolina. It is designed to stop the government from giving special gifts or subsidies to private individuals when these grants will contribute no real benefit to the public at large. Would payment of "tuition grants" to private persons to finance their personal education in private schools—schools subject to little state supervision—constitute the expenditure of public revenue for a "public purpose"?

The question is difficult because the courts have never defined the term "public purpose" with any precise certainty. In earlier times—indeed, perhaps up to the 1930's—the courts usually took a strict view of novel types of expenditures of government funds when these expenditures resulted in placing a sizeable sum in the palms of only a few private persons. In the last quarter of the 19th century, a number of cases arose in the state courts which involved the question of whether governmental grants to specific private educational organizations constituted expenditure of public money for a "public purpose." The courts rather uniformly invalidated these expenditures, principally on the grounds that: (a) no governmental control was exercised over the management of the private school recipients, (b) the schools were not available for use by the public at large—or even a segment of the public, and (c) the public schools rather than private schools should be the beneficiaries of any expenditures to advance education.

These precedents, if followed today, might prompt the courts to invalidate "tuition grants" to children on the theory that the grants served no "public purpose." But it is possible that the courts would distinguish the earlier precedents. And it is worth noting that judicial notions about the "public purpose" served by subsidies to private individuals have generally become more liberal. This, after all, is an age of subsidies, and there are many in the field of education: the G. I. Bill of Rights, the Fulbright scholarships and numerous other governmental grants are illustrative. Presumably, today, a court would be reluctant to cast doubts on the legality of these ventures. There is also a trend to adhere closer to the general principle that great "deference" must be paid to the legislature's determination of what constitutes a "public purpose." This idea is especially noticeable in some recent Supreme Court cases.

There exists of course a possibility that "tuition grants" might be struck down as invalid of the "public purpose" doctrine because the schools which eventually receive the money are subject to no regulation by the State, and thus there can be no assurance that the State will get its money's worth when it supplies the child with tuition funds. This is a necessary risk under the "tuition grant" plan. If the State carefully regulated the schools, it might thereby assure that the "tuition grant" expenditures would involve a "public purpose," but this would increase the likelihood that the schools would become subject to the Fourteenth Amendment. Even without any state regulation, there is a possibility that the operation of the private schools involved in the "tuition grant" plan would involve "state action."

The "State Action" Problem. The plan now discussed contemplates an absolute minimum of state participation in an effort to organize and maintain *free* private schools. However, state funds would contribute to the support of the schools; indeed, in that sense the State would, presumably, be the exclusive source of money for the financial maintenance of most of the schools. Would this mean that the school was a state activity?

No court has said—and it may be unlikely that any ever will say—that any and all economic assistance, no matter how trivial, coming from a state to a private organization will automatically subject that organization to the limitations of the Fourteenth Amendment. On the other hand, assume outright grants, directly appropriated to a private institution, and assume that these grants comprise the major source of operating revenue of the institution. When the State exerts that much sovereign power to support the private institution, the likelihood of a judicial finding that the operation of the institution involves "state action" is greater.

A decision of the United States Court of Appeals for the Fourth Circuit indicates this. The Court considered the status of a library in Baltimore, Maryland. This library was originally created by private endowment; it was managed by private trustees, but it was also heavily supported by direct appropriation of public funds from the city. It operated a training school for librarians which was closed to Negro applicants. The library claimed that it was free to exclude Negroes if it chose because it was a private institution. But the Court overruled the claim. The decision declared that the city's financial support was an obvious exertion of state authority in behalf of the library; consequently the operation of the library involved "state action," and the exclusion of Negroes by the library's school was "state action" in violation of the Fourteenth Amendment.

The library case, of course, does not settle our private school problem. The "tuition grant" private school plan presents a situation where the state grants are not handed over directly to a particular named institution. The State, ostensibly at least, gives the money to the *parents*, not the schools. Because no money goes direct from the State to the schools, the courts might say that the school was no state activity. Indeed, it is arguable that a contrary decision might possibly have significant reper-

cussions on the effect of receipt of any G. I. Bill tuition by any privately owned university. But the G. I. Bill financed college and the "tuition grant" financed private school may become distinguishable situations when we examine other aspects of the "tuition grant" plan.

For we must be aware of the total background in which the private schools operating under this plan would exist. If the "tuition grant" proposal were adopted, there would probably be many, many private schools—all operating by the grace of state "tuition grants"—throughout the State; and these presumably would be the schools which would fulfill the function of educating a large segment of the white population in the State.

So the Court might take note of both the purpose and the end result achieved by these free private schools. Mindful of the fact that supplying free education in state schools has come to be "perhaps the most important function of state and local government," the Court might hold that when the State provides for an alternative method—when the State in effect delegates the business of supplying *free* education to all private schools which volunteer for the task— this renders each private school subject to the limitations of the Fourteenth Amendment.

And the kindred principle reflected in the trade union cases—that a private organization cannot use special privileges granted it by the state to work a planned discrimination— might also have some applicability here. The schools receive state money; it comes to the schools via the parents, but it is, in a sense, earmarked for the schools and, in this instance, money is power—the power to provide free education. There exists at least some doubt that such power, when it is given to a private group by the State, can be wielded in a fashion to accomplish results which the State is forbidden to accomplish itself.

The only safe generalization to make in adjudging the existence of "state action" is to say that it is probably a "matter of degree." That is of small comfort. But it does caution that to be successful, a private school plan would probably have to involve an absolute minimum of state financing and governing of the schools and no assistance in the physical creation of the schools. This in turn may be of some help to those

who must make the ultimate decision whether to embark on such a program, for it poses the unavoidable question of whether the game is worth the candle.

Could Tuition Grants Be Paid to Children Attending Church Schools? The "tuition grant" plan contemplates no effort by the State to aid in the establishment of private schools. This means that the task of organizing and managing the schools would be left to the initiative of the community.

It has been suggested that local churches could undertake this task, for they might have the organization and the wherewithal to launch a new private school.

But if the State should propose to pay a child's way through a church school, in lieu of sending him to public school, it would in a sense be putting itself in the business of financing sectarian education. And it is well-established that no government, federal or state, can grant money outright to any parochial schools or to any churches. This principle is embedded in the First Amendment to the Constitution of the United States. In the words of the Court:

> The "establishment of religion" clause of the First Amendment means at least this: Neither a state nor the Federal Government can set up a church. Neither can pass laws which aid one religion, aid all religions, or prefer one religion over another. Neither can force nor influence a person to go to or to remain away from church against his will or force him to profess a belief in any religion. No person can be punished for entertaining or professing religious beliefs or disbeliefs, for church attendance or non-attendance. *No tax in any amount, large or small, can be levied to support any religious activities or institutions, whatever they may be called or whatever form they may adopt to teach or practice religion.* Neither a state nor the Federal Government can, openly or secretly, participate in the affairs of any religious organizations or groups and *vice versa.* In the words of Jefferson, the clause against establishment of religion by law was intended to erect "a wall of separation between church and State." (Emphasis added.)

The decision quoted above suggests a firm constitutional principle against any outright grants to church schools or financing any sectarian education. This and other recent decisions raise some doubts that any state has the constitutional power to support church schools through grants to pay for the tuition of the pupils who choose to attend those schools.

The Public Schools And the Next Decision

Perhaps the private school plans won't withstand constitutional attack. Perhaps the plans will be thought impracticable. Perhaps the public education system should be preserved. Assuming that North Carolina does choose to retain its public school system, what action may it take to meet the law of the Brown decision and yet make the easiest possible adjustment to the difficulties which may lie ahead?

The question is hard to answer because the Court has not yet declared *how* or *when* the constitutional rights which it has adjudicated may be enforced by those Negroes who seek to enforce them. Presumably the task of establishing that law will be undertaken when the Court renders its next decision.

North Carolina's Attorney General has been invited to participate in the forthcoming argument. The question now considered is not: Should he appear? There is no intent to suggest here that the State's only course is to have its Attorney General go before the Court. Rather the question to be treated is: *If* the Attorney General does appear, what principles could he argue for which will be of use to this State in resolving the problems spawned by the Brown decision? In other words: Without arguing in favor of participation by this State in the next argument, let us just *assume*, for present purposes, that the Attorney General might choose to go to Washington this fall; and let us ask: What might be accomplished by taking that step?

The Attorney General might be able to persuade the Court to recognize several very important broad, general principles. These broad principles might make it possible to work out an adjustment to the Brown decision which would *not* be so revolutionary to the State's institutions as may have been anticipated. These cornerstone principles have to do with: (1) the time element, (2) state discretion, (3) geographical variation within a state in adopting measures to meet the decision, (4) preventing racial antipathy from jeopardizing the proper functions of the schools, (5) preserving the academic

standards in the schools, and (6) preserving the health and personal security of the children who attend the schools.

1. The Time Element

Ordinarily, whenever a person suffers an abridgment of his legal rights, he is entitled to an immediate remedy. In the segregation cases now pending the plaintiffs originally asked for such judicial action. However, the Court has set down, for reargument, the question of whether there should be a "gradual adjustment" to its ruling. This may be a hint that the Court could be persuaded to allow a period of time in which the states can work out slowly whatever changes are necessary.

How long? There is no express inference of an answer to this. "Gradual adjustment" might signify a period of at least three, perhaps five, perhaps twelve, perhaps more years. But it is quite possible that the Court will not fix any *precise* time limit at all. Rather, the time might be left *indefinite*; the only limitation on the school authorities might be this: That they make *reasonable progress*; so long as they do make progress, the date for final completion of the task of "de-segregation" will be left open.

There are, to be sure, some tough arguments to be advanced against this principle.

In a number of prior cases involving segregation at the graduate school level, where Negro applicants to white graduate schools were able to prove that there were no "equal" outside facilities for Negroes which would afford them the same educational opportunity, the Court ordered *immediate admittance* of the Negroes to the "white" schools. The Court has declared: Rights under the Fourteenth Amendment are "personal and present." "Personal" means that each individual has a right of his own to "equal protection." "Present" means that there can be no delay about giving him "equal protection." From this it probably will be argued that "gradual adjustment" would be a repudiation of existing law, that the Court should stick to the prior procedure of granting some sort of immediate relief. And it can be argued, too, that any scheme of "gradual adjustment" will be but a dodge—a law of compliance which permits state officials to do nothing at all whenever they are of a disposition to do nothing. Those are some of the argu-

ments which may be marshalled against "gradual adjustment."

On the other hand, the earlier segregation cases could be distinguished; they involved a very different situation. Each of them involved suits by single individuals for admission into graduate schools; the present cases involve suits by hundreds of Negro school children, and these plaintiffs would be the first to admit, because they have assumed it all along in these "test" cases, that there are thousands, even millions of other Negro students, whose rights are also going to be immediately affected by any decree which the Court might enter. Comparatively speaking, it is easy for a university to admit one Negro in a graduate school; it is extremely difficult, even disregarding the factor of racial antipathy, for public schools to shift pupils around according to a new system which will take no account of race.

In the earlier decisions, when the Court ordered admission of the Negroes, it made no major revision of the meaning of "equal protection." No significant change in a state's whole school system was necessitated. Quite the contrary in the present cases. The decision may affect administration, expenditures, the allocation of pupils and teachers, and so forth, to a very great extent. It may necessitate revision of state statutes. Changes of this kind can never be worked overnight.

When confronted with other big, complicated cases in different areas of the law, the Court has often allowed a considerable transition period to work out relief. Notable instances of this have occurred in the antitrust field.

It boils down to this: The plaintiffs in the segregation cases have in effect argued heretofore that they represent Negroes wherever segregation is practiced; they have deliberately raised a case which unavoidably affects well-established conditions in at least seventeen states; the five cases were submitted on that theory; the first decision was rendered on that assumption; and the second—addressing itself to remedies—can hardly ignore the far-reaching effect of the first. Indeed, language in the Court's opinion takes note of the difficulties just discussed. And the Court's invitation to the states implicitly carries recognition of the many, many problems involved in fashioning a remedy. It seems certain that the Court invited the states to appear—not as a matter of form—

but because each state can and should have an opportunity to demonstrate the many diverse obstacles to adjustment to the *Brown* decision.

2. The Element of Discretion

"Gradual adjustment" may also imply another fundamental principle in the law of compliance. This principle, too, may be of significant value to the State in resolving its problems.

There is a possibility that the Court could be persuaded to establish a principle for "gradual adjustment" which will leave great discretion as to ways and means in the responsible state school authorities. Perhaps it can be persuaded to formulate law which will provide roughly that the federal courts should stay their hands *completely* until the school authorities have first devised and inaugurated a plan reasonable on its face. Only if these measures prove to be patently invalid, or only if nothing is attempted by the school authorities after a reasonable length of time, should the courts intervene.

We are dealing with an extraordinary situation. The unusual features of the segregation cases have already been depicted. Vital public interests of the states are involved— e.g., expenditures of revenue, assignment of teachers and allocation of facilities. In the face of all this, it is not hard to imagine that the Court will be extremely reluctant to involve either itself or the lower federal courts in the intricate, time-consuming business of managing schools. That sort of task has always been left to the hands of administrative agencies, not the courts. The Supreme Court has in recent years, in effect, often told the lower courts: When you are confronted with an intricate case involving activity which is subject to regulation by a special agency, then you must follow a "hands off" policy until the administrative agencies have first had a chance to act. The immediate defendants in the school cases are school boards—administrative agencies which have been established by state laws to manage the state schools. The problems they face are intricate, to say the least. The school boards have not yet had a chance to act on these problems. Perhaps the Court can be persuaded to tell the lower courts in effect: Hands off; let the school boards have a chance to work out the difficult problems of adjustment to the *Brown* decision.

The precedents which apply here are not based on rigid rules of law.

They are discretionary limits on the exercise of judicial power by the federal courts. But the "hands off" policy has been particularly applicable when the Court is dealing with *state* agencies. So these "hands off" cases may supply important precedents in the next decision in the "segregation cases," which pose a most difficult problem of relations between sovereignties under our federal system of government.

Finally, one more point. In resolving the second decision, the Court is *now* empowered by statute to enter any "appropriate judgment, decree or order or require such further proceedings to be had as may be just under the circumstances." Statutory language could hardly devise a broader or more flexible grant of power to work out a pattern of adjustment along the lines indicated in this study.

3. Geographical Variations in Approach and in Timing among Different Localities within the State

North Carolina's Negro population varies widely in density throughout the State. This, presumably, may produce considerable differences in the problems now confronting the various communities of the State. Take two extremes: In some cities or counties full implementation of the principle of the *Brown* decision might produce, comparatively speaking, little change in the make-up of the schools; by reason of a normal redistricting of attendance areas, or by reason of a small Negro population there might be few Negro pupils to be shifted to white schools. Yet in some other areas the decision may affect many pupils; the impact of any sudden change might have severe consequences. Again, in some areas it may seem feasible to use one method of designating the schools to be attended by each student, in other areas a totally different approach might be desirable. In some areas it may take far longer to work out the adjustment than in others.

The Court might be persuaded to recognize this need for geographical variation.

Beyond question a state need not provide for territorial uniformity in methods of governing every locality within its borders. And the *Brown* decision—while it forbids a total enforced separation of students based solely on their race—does not compel any one method of designating which school a pupil must attend; indeed, as we have already seen, it would seem possible that the Court will

still allow complete discretion to the state school authorities in working out a slow adjustment to a system which no longer requires segregation solely for reasons of race. School officials should be able to pick and choose between methods; and quite probably some schools could make a slower start and slower progress than others—depending upon local conditions.

Note that we are here talking, not about a system which permits some local school boards to deny constitutional rights while others do not, but about a system which permits a variance in the *remedial period* for working out an adjustment to meet the *Brown* decision. Plain and simply, it is but a fact of life that there can be no uniform pace of adjustment. The *Brown* opinion takes note of differences in problems between the various states which now adhere to segregation, and the facts to illustrate these differences were well-developed in the records of all five school segregation cases. It may be relatively easy to "de-segregate" in a state like Kansas, because that state, itself, has already abolished segregation in most of its schools. Obviously, it would not be easy to tackle the problem in Clarendon County, South Carolina, where the number of Negro students is far larger than the number of white students. This points up the likelihood that the Court will allow both considerable state discretion and considerable state variance in meeting its first decision. And if variance between states is permissible, local variance within states, in timing and in method, should also be possible.

4. Taking Account of the Intensity of Racial Feeling

Assume, though it may be hoped that the assumption is unfounded, that a major difficulty in adjustment in some areas will be the possibility of serious disruption of the school program if white and colored children are immediately intermingled to any great extent.

For example: Suppose a particular community has a large Negro school population. Suppose that a change-over to a school system where race plays no part whatsoever in the assignment of children to school would mean that some schools would have a very high proportion of Negroes to whites. And suppose that this possibility would arouse considerable community hostility to the change. Finally, suppose that all this would clearly spell serious interference with the school's program if such a change were undertaken. To handle this situation the school authorities might wish to delay making immediate, abrupt changes. They might wish to take steps to integrate only a few Negro students with white students—rather than plan a change to a pattern where the number of Negroes will be so great that disorder may well ensue.

This approach might be possible under the law if the Court would recognize the factor of racial feeling and permit the states to take account of it in certain circumstances. True, the possibility of physical disturbancs in the schools did not stop the Court from deciding that the bi-racial, separate school system must be abolished. But does it necessarily follow that this possibility should be ignored in decreeing what is to be the *remedy* to segregation? As already noted, the Court has wide, flexible powers in respect to the remedy. An essential criterion in the exercise of these powers is to do justice. This includes the power to fashion a remedy that will secure compliance with the law and yet still accommodate, to the fullest possible extent, the needs and interests of all students. A remedy which would precipitate immediate violence or frustration of the activities of the schools in some areas (where the proportion of Negro students to white is high) would hardly fit the needs of any school children. In those places a remedy; which recognizes the illegality of segregation but delays any great changes until some initial experimentation with non-separation and until some conditioning to the idea can be achieved, might suit the "needs" of all parties far more. If the facts to prove this argument can be properly brought before the Supreme Court, it might recognize the special necessity for a "go slow" approach in trouble areas.

Nor does it necessarily follow that this principle would import too vague a standard and would too easily be invoked as a dodge. Standards for administering it could be made reasonably precise. The principle could require a finding that serious frustration of the functioning of the schools would be the result of immediate mixed attendance. A determination to this effect would require convincing evidence, not idle speculation. It might require that reference be made to the community's history of racial relations, to the *bona fide* be-

liefs of responsible citizens, to other relevant considerations demonstrating the likelihood of strife, but, above all, to · the population factor. Nor could findings to this effect justify a continuing total failure to take any steps towards adjustment to a school system which took no account of color. Some experimental efforts to prepare for change should eventually be practiced, for example: integration of some younger classes in some smaller schools where the classes and behavior will be easier to control and where the proportion of Negro to white students will not be high.

5. Taking Account of Differences in Academic Backgrounds between Negro and White Students

The Court might be persuaded to recognize still another ground for the "go slow" approach.

If local authorities could demonstrate that pupils of one race in a given grade could *not* be expected to participate and keep up with students of the other race in the same grade level, then it is arguable that immediate integration ·of the two classes would be unreasonable and delay justifiable. Preservation of the academic standards of the schools is an interest which the Court should permit the states to protect. This may mean some delays in making changes. Obviously such delays could only be temporary. And they should be permissible. There might be obvious ill effects, both on the students and the school system, if children of the same grade level but with wholly different academic backgrounds were immediately intermingled.

Again, to forestall contentions that delay for this reason would amount to deliberate evasions, there would exist a need for detailed and impartial analysis of the facts by the school authorities. They should do that to justify the delay. And it is to be noted that at the lower grade levels in school, the disparity in academic background between Negro and white pupils might be less evident. So it may be doubted that, in · the absence of unusual conditions, school authorities could invoke this particular principle to justify a delay in de-segregating the lower grade levels of the schools.

6. Taking Account of the Need to Protect the Health of Individual Students

The right of a child to attend school without restriction as to race—like

the right of a person to practice his religion free from governmental restriction—should not override the well-established constitutional power of a state to take measures clearly designed to prevent the spread of disease. But the power to protect health cannot be used indiscriminately. The Court has previously noted that the "equal protection" clause is a limitation against the power of the states to single out, indiscriminately, some "particular race or nationality for oppressive treatment" on the grounds that they are fit objects for special precautionary health measures. It is a question of adopting means which are limited to dealing with the particular danger at hand. Thus, just because one child of a particular race, if allowed to mix freely with all children, might be a menace to the health of all does not mean that every child of his race may be singled out for the same treatment.

7. Taking Account of the Personality, Needs and Desires of Individual Children

A number of "de-segregation" plans proposed and practiced in other parts of the country have taken note of the difficulty involved in dislocating great numbers of students from a school and an environment in which they are well-established and removing them to a new environment. As set forth in a plan adopted for Washington, D: C.: "stability, continuity and security in the educational experiences of the pupils during the transition period" are overriding factors; and it may be that any plan for gradual adjustment should seek, insofar as possible, to accommodate these interests. Surely a central idea behind the notion of "gradual adjustment" is to take account of precisely this facet of the problem.

To be more precise: Suppose that a local school authority, to adjust to the *Brown* decision, works out a re-districting of its school areas and a re-allocation of pupils to school facilities. But by virtue of this change a student who would, under the old system, attend high school "A" would now be eligible for transfer to high school "B." The transfer may uproot him from friends and a school community and environment where he is well-established. It may even thrust him into a school where there are few other members of his race. Be he Negro or white, neither he nor his parents may wish for the change. Under such circumstances could he be permitted an election—a choice between moving to school "B" which is now designated to serve his neighborhood, or remaining in school "A" where he is well-established?

In practice, of course, such a plan might well result in a considerable amount of voluntary segregation. But that does not automatically violate the law of the Brown case. The Brown case established a constitutional right for Negro school children—the right to be free of compulsory segregation on the grounds of race. Yet it is well-established that a person can waive his constitutional rights. And the states can provide for such a waiver. Certainly permitting such a waiver might be allowed here, when the purpose of the waiver is to cushion the race-relations impact on children of a decision which, after all, has its sharpest impact on children and not adults.

8. Summary and Comment

Nothing in the Brown opinion suggests that the Supreme Court of the United States is hellbent to force immediate integration upon the states which have for years operated segregated schools without any court declaration to the effect that the practice violated "the Supreme Law of the Land." And, as already noted, there are indications that the Court may well be quite receptive to arguments which will depict, graphically, that which the Court cannot know fully without instruction—the nature of the problems now confronting states affected by the Brown decision. Recognizing these problems, the Court may well respond favorably to proposals for underlying broad principles of the "law of compliance" which are calculated to ease these difficulties.

Accordingly, it would seem that one initial step this State might take to meet the Brown decision is to appear before the Court and fight for the largest possible expansion of the framework of law which would allow a "gradual adjustment" to the decision—an expansion which would allow much time and much discretion to school authorities to implement the law the Court has propounded in its first decision. There has been no purpose to argue that the State should, or that it must, take this step; the purpose is simply to outline the possibilities of obtaining a decision which will establish law permitting such gradual adjustment.

It is worth noting that the initial step—trying to persuade the Court to recognize the need for a gradual adjustment—will not tie the State's hands in the future in any way. Appearing before the Court will not commit this State to any particular "plan" of compliance. Appearing before the Court will not mean that the Court's forthcoming decrees will operate against the schools of this State; the Court, beyond question has no power to make the State a defendant in the five cases now before it; nor did the Court invite the State to submit its entire school system to the Court's jurisdiction. It did not ask the State to submit any "plan" for compliance; it simply asked the State to appear as an "amicus curiae," i.e., in an advisory capacity, to help inform the Court as to the difficulties involved in implementing its decision. Of course, it would probably avail little to go before the Court and simply tell it, in effect, to reverse itself. The Brown decision is the law of the land, and the Court made its decision only after long and deliberate consideration. For better or worse the Court has spoken, and what's been done can hardly be undone. Yet the next decision may be quite crucial. The next decision—dealing with the "how" and the "when" of enforcing the first—will also be the law of the land in that it may well set the pattern and establish the practices which the states may follow in adjusting to "de-segregation." In that sense, North Carolina will be bound by the second decision, and it will be bound whether or not it boycotts the Court. Thus, the next decision may be crucial, and an appearance by the State, coupled with the most persuasive arguments which the State could make, might help to produce a second decision which will reduce the difficulty of some of the problems which now seem so catastrophic and so imminent to so many communities in North Carolina.

Possible Ways of Working a "Gradual Adjustment"

We have seen that it is possible that the Court, because of the extraordinary nature of its decision, may be persuaded to formulate law which will

(1) Give the State a long—perhaps indefinite—time to adjust its school system to the law of the Brown decision,

(2) Leave the State free to devise its own ways and means to

work the adjustment without court interference,

(3) Permit geographical variations within the State in ways and means and timing,

(4) Permit the school authorities to take limited but appropriate measures to prevent mixed attendance from resulting in such conditions as:

(a) Racial antipathies seriously impairing the proper functioning of the schools;

(b) Serious impairment of the academic standards of the schools;

(c) Threat to the health or psychological security of individual students who might be affected by a change in schools.

Let us assume that the Court will recognize these principles. How could they be used to devise methods of designating a school to be attended by each child in North Carolina who is educated in the public school system? The answer is that there are a number of methods which local school authorities, in their discretion, might use.

1. Assignment

One way which the responsible school authorities might choose to deal with the school placement problem is by making individual assignments. Thus the placement of each child who resides within the jurisdiction of a local school board could be treated as an individual case. The board could weigh all the standards listed above and then assign the child to a particular school.

For example: The board might seek to estimate, first, the effect which mixed attendance might have upon the functioning of the schools in its particular community. If the proportion of Negro students to whites is high, if feeling runs strong against any abrupt change in school placement which would mingle students according to this proportion, if this antipathy is strong enough to constitute a serious threat to the functioning of the schools, then, according to the principles already laid down, the board could take steps to limit mixed attendance. In fact, as noted, where conditions were sufficiently aggravated, it could use its assignment power to attempt experiments in mixed attendance only at some selected schools or only at certain grade levels. And it could also invoke other standards noted above

—academic background and psychological needs of pupils—to select for experiments in mixed attendance only those pupils who might best adjust to the change.

The board would be empowered to "feel its way" through the problem. The obvious limitation on this power is, in non-legal language, that it use *good faith and common sense to make progress*. It must be remembered that it is the law of the *Brown* case that enforced separation has been declared illegal. And we are now talking about the exercise of the assignment power as a transitional means to adjust to this law, rather than as a method to preserve the status quo, permanently and totally.

But could the assignment power be used to effectuate total segregation, permanently? That suggestion has been made. And legislation in at least two states has apparently been framed for this purpose. The statutes provide that the assignment of each child to a public school is to be treated as an individual case requiring a separate decision on the part of the responsible agency. The assignment is to be based upon such factors as the "welfare" of the child, or "the best interests" of the child, the "health" of the schools and the "welfare and best interests of the schools involved."

Judged in the abstract, all of these proposed assignment plans appear to be legal. But that is no end to the matter. For if they were tested in a case arising against a background of a consistent practice of racial segregation—especially a background of statewide, total racial segregation on the part of local school boards, this ostensible legality would probably not save the plan from invalidation by the courts. The nub of the matter is that the *Brown* decision declares that race can no longer be used as a governing standard in the assignment of children to schools. The decision has necessarily rejected the view that total, permanent racial segregation is a legitimate way of exercising the states' admitted power to protect the "welfare" of students and the "best interests" of schools.

Nor would it matter that the assignment statute appeared to be valid on its face because it made no express provision for racial segregation; if, in fact, the action of an assignment board were challenged in a case which arose against a background of total,

permanent segregation, and not gradual adjustment, the courts would quite probably *not* be deterred from entertaining damage suits against the board, invalidating its action and ordering charges. The Supreme Court has declared:

> . . . Though [a] law itself be fair on its face and impartial in appearance, yet, if it is applied and administered by public authority with an evil eye and an unequal hand, so as practically to make unjust and illegal discriminations between persons in similar circumstances, material to their rights, the denial of equal justice is still within the prohibition of the Constitution.

This oft-quoted language means that persistent, discriminatory enforcement of non-discriminatory statutes may render the enforcing agency subject to the corrective power of the courts. Thus, once it might become apparent that an assignment statute was being administered so as "to make . . . illegal discriminations"—discriminations which the school authorities had no legal power to make— then a court might well feel free to take whatever steps it deemed necessary to halt the practice of using valid assignment criteria to accomplish an illegal result—permanent and total segregation rather than gradual adjustment. This would be especially true if an assignment plan were openly advertised as a device for insuring total, permanent segregation.

Summary. Perhaps it boils down to this: Certain broad standards governing "gradual adjustment" have been outlined and summarized above. If the State could persuade the Court to recognize the legality of those standards, then the power to assign children to school could be used to experiment with gradual adjustment, and to continue separate schools in part, where conditions exist which would justify separation under those standards. But it would be a far different case, were the school officials to ignore those standards and simply adopt the assignment method to compel permanent and total statewide separation—especially where t h a t purpose is openly advertised to all the world. The first method would seem to be a permissible means of "gradual adjustment." But the second method of assignment—i.e., using valid criteria to compel total, permanent segregation, and not gradual adjustment—seems to have been invalidated by the *Brown* decision itself.

2. Redistricting

Another way of determining which school a child must attend is to district the school system into attendance areas. Each child living in a particular geographical district attends the school designated to serve his area.

Obviously, this is a permissible means of determining school placement. It assures efficient utilization of existing school facilities; it may also serve to protect the health and safety of children by permitting them to attend those schools which are located nearest to their residences. Of course, use of this method may serve to separate the races into different schools in those places where Negro and white populations are now concentrated into separate geographical areas and where schools are conveniently located to serve each of these areas. But the fact that "segregation" may result where such conditions obtain would hardly constitute a violation of the law of the *Brown* decision.

It is even arguable that the courts will never interfere with *any* redistricting; that they will never inquire into the fairness of the boundaries, and will never listen to any claim that an alleged "gerrymandering" has resulted in a denial of "equal protection." That argument might refer to cases which have arisen involving the "gerrymandering" of legislative and congressional districts. In those cases the Supreme Court has rather consistently—but as a matter of discretion only, and not pursuant to any rigid rule of law—refused to order lower courts to undertake the task of redrawing the lines of voting districts to make them comport with the plaintiff's notions of a more proportional representation.

Yet there is nothing magic about attendance areas which necessarily immunizes them from judicial scrutiny. It is important to note that the process of establishing attendance areas is but a way—one method—of assigning children to school; it is but a form of the assignment power. And we have already seen that the assignment power cannot be exercised in a discriminatory fashion to maintain *total, permanent* segregation in all the schools. That seems to be the heart and substance of the *Brown* decision. And open resort to racially districted attendance areas to achieve total, permanent segregation differs little in substance from resort to any other valid standards of the assignment power to achieve an illegal result. In sum: the very arguments noted in connection with assignment may be invoked here to attack school attendance areas which have been redistricted completely along racial lines by obvious "gerrymandering."

However, the courts would probably be reluctant to involve themselves in many cases involving alleged "gerrymandering" of school attendance areas. Granting relief in such cases will invite constant litigation; every time the boundaries of a district are slightly revised, even if no racial exclusion was intended, a dissatisfied parent might rush into court complaining of a "gerrymander." Drawing district lines involves many factors which courts often refuse to review; such decisions (to use the terminology of the courts) pose "political" or "legislative" problems—matters which the courts have traditionally refused to consider. So where the attendance areas are at least reasonably related in terms of geographical proximity to the schools which serve the city or county, the courts might refuse to interfere.

But where it is shown that a county or a city has a sizeable Negro population, and where it is shown that the distribution of this Negro population lies *not* in one compact area close by one school but rather that colored families are scattered all over the area—where these conditions are shown, and where it is also shown that all Negroes have been somehow districted into separate attendance areas, then a presumption of illegality might arise sufficient to prompt a court to take jurisdiction over the case.

Summary. Re-districting of attendance areas to assure continued efficient utilization of existing school facilities is certainly a valid exercise of state power. So far as "gerrymandering" is concerned it would seem to be a matter of degree. The doctrines which have prompted a hands-off policy in other types of "gerrymandering" do not necessarily apply to school attendance areas. Yet the courts would probably be reluctant to involve themselves in any except extreme cases.

3. School Election

As already indicated the Court might well recognize, as a general principle of "gradual adjustment," the need to accommodate the personal desires and security of students most affected by any change in school placement wrought by the law of the Brown case. This suggests that, at least during a transitional period of adjustment, the courts might well permit a system of school selection based on choice.

Of course, such a system, if used on a wide basis, might prove unmanageable and subject to abuse; a general referendum of all students in a large area might partake of the attributes of a "Saar election." But in some situations it might be both desirable and workable. Thus, in some areas where, after a re-districting, Negro children fall within the attendance area served by a traditionally white school (and a school to be attended mostly by white children), or where white children fall within the area served by a traditionally colored school (and a school to be attended mostly by colored children), the pupils immediately affected by this change might be allowed a choice of schools. Or, to employ a slight variation, one attendance area might be marked out which would be served by two schools —a school which had been traditionally Negro and a school which had been traditionally white; and children living within this area might be allowed a choice to attend either of the two schools. If there is validity in the prediction, which has often been made in the wake of the Brown decision, that a majority in both races will, if left to their own volition, separate themselves, then voluntary segregation will be the result of the choice; and many of the difficulties which might ensue from mixed attendance will be overcome.

Would such a system of school selection be valid? In the light of what has already been said, it would certainly seem valid as a transitional measure. And quite possibly it might be valid as a permanent measure. To be sure, some strong arguments might be directed against such "voluntary separation": it might be said that the system is designed in practice to permit white persons to separate themselves, and Negro students, who desire to exercise their "equal protection" rights to attend a mixed school, may do so only by incurring community disapproval and only by electing to attend a school which the white persons in the community have deliberately chosen to set apart for themselves.

Yet the plan makes no express provision for the imposition of such a "burden" on Negro children desiring integration. It avoids all references —and this is important—to maintaining any separate schools for the races; it does not single out Negroes as the class of persons who must make the choice, alone; rather all children choose on equal terms; whatever separation of the races occurs is entirely the product of volition and nothing else; the State will have done nothing to promote it in an active sense. Again, there might be a serious question as to whether any Negro student would have legal standing to raise a case to challenge the plan in the courts.

Of course, if the school choice plan were advertised openly as a way of insuring *permanent* and *total* segregation, and if coercive means were continuously applied, year after year, to insure that the choice of each Negro child would be but a choice to separate himself from the white children—if that were the context in which the plan should be challenged in the courts, then there might be a very serious question as to its validity. A Negro—even one who was allowed to attend a white school— might then have standing to attack the plan. He could argue: True, the State has not forcibly segregated me, but it has exerted pressure to force me and others of my race to separate ourselves; the exertion of such pressure is but a modified form of precisely the exertion of state power which was invalidated in the Brown decision—the power to require colored children, because of their race, to attend separate schools.

Indeed, even if the state officials winked at purely private action to effect segregation and accepted the choice of a student who had been subjected to pressure by private persons and not public officials, this too might give rise to a possible case of "state action" in violation of "equal protection." Certainly that argument would be fortified the moment it could be shown that the plan—the provision for this machinery of election between two schools—was adopted for the very purpose of preserving the *status quo* of segregation.

At this point it may be well to discuss two other proposals for voluntary segregation. Both are apparently designed to achieve total, permanent segregation.

1. First, there might be a plan which would incorporate these fea-

tures: All school-aged Negro children would be asked: "Do you wish to attend your former school, or do you wish to attend school with white children?" If an overwhelming majority (e.g., 75% or more) elect the Negro school, then all Negroes should be requested (or perhaps required) to attend that school. Thus, this plan contemplates total segregation where a heavy majority of Negroes favor total segregation.

But the difficulty with this argument lies in the fact that the State would be subjecting constitutional rights to a majority vote. The *Brown* decision establishes a Fourteenth Amendment right for Negro children. It is the right to attend public schools without being segregated because of their race. Constitutional rights can never be abrogated by a majority vote. Rights established by the Fourteenth Amendment have long been characterized as "personal." As the Court has said, this means that each Negro student, "as an individual" and not as a member of a class, is "entitled to the 'equal protection' of the laws . . . Whether or not other Negroes [have] sought the same [educational] opportunity."

2. A second plan, one which seems to contemplate much permanent segregation proposes the following: All students would be given a choice; white students will elect between an all-white or an integrated school; Negro students will elect between an all-Negro or an integrated school. The legality of the plan is questionable because it permits enforced separation of the races. It provides that members of one race *must* be excluded from some schools which are openly set apart to members of the other race alone. Negroes are totally and permanently excluded from certain schools solely because of their race. Thus the plan contemplates maintaining segregated schools, and this exertion of state power may well run squarely into the law of the *Brown* decision. That decision seems to forbid any such permanent enforced segregation of the races.

Summary. Much space has been devoted to discussing the possibility that some methods of voluntary segregation may be illegal. But this should not obscure the fact that other methods of school choice might withstand constitutional attack, if these plans were fairly administered (e.g., without allowing coercion to dictate the child's choice). Thus if the plan were simply that each and every child were allowed to attend the school of his choice, if there were no strings and no coercion, then the school election system would seem unassailable. This may be especially true if the plan were adopted as a transitional device to assure "gradual adjustment."

4. A System of Administrative Appeals

Thus far three systems of school placement have been discussed. The theory has been set forth that local school officials in their discretion might utilize any one of these methods or perhaps a combination of any or all of them to meet the problems of their particular community. The theory has been that there need be no uniformity of method among local boards in meeting these problems but rather that considerable flexibility and discretion should exist at the local level. This *ad hoc* local approach to the school problem need entail no radical revision of the State's present school system; it should require no abandonment of the "state" system of education.

On the contrary, the State Board might be empowered to exercise a review power over the operations of local boards.

It is a well-established principle of law that one who complains of the effects of a particular governmental action must first exhaust all administrative remedies. This doctrine has been applied in the field of constitutional law. Where a plaintiff seeks court action against a claimed infringement of his constitutional rights, he must first demonstrate that he has sought relief, unsuccessfully, from every administrative agency empowered by law to give him relief from the alleged injury. Accordingly, it might be appropriate to devise a "state" system of administrative appeals to review decisions of local school boards. In other words, provide that every parent dissatisfied with the local board's action in regard to placing students in school would have to go before the State Board before being allowed to sue the local board in the courts.

This step would be consistent with North Carolina's Constitution and with the traditional organization of the State's school system. Second, it might enable the Board to assure that there would be a wise and efficient use of school properties and school funds throughout the State. Third, it might serve as an added deterrent both to unwarranted litigation and harassment in the operation of the schools.

5. Institutions of Higher Learning

There can be little doubt but that the *Brown* decision controls not only segregated schools but also segregated universities. There can be little doubt but that the courts will rule that exclusion from a state-operated university solely on the grounds of race now constitutes a violation of the applicant's constitutional right to "equal protection of the laws."

We have already referred to the several graduate school cases where the courts ordered admission of colored applicants to white universities despite the fact that state law required their exclusion. In those cases the courts found that the exclusion violated the Fourteenth Amendment, not because segregation was *per se* unconstitutional, but because the applicants were seeking certain educational advantages which were available at the time only within the white university. Further, the Court characterized the right of the Negro applicant as "personal and present," and this meant: *immediate admission.*

Arguments have heretofore been advanced that the "personal and present" doctrine may be modified or suspended when it comes to enforcing rights of Negro children in the public schools. These arguments were predicated upon the assumption that the *Brown* decision thrusts extraordinary administrative and race-relations difficulties upon those responsible for the management of the schools. If those charged with management of the colleges can show that they, too, are confronted with problems of similar magnitude, then the courts might also make provision for gradual adjustment in those institutions rather than immediate implementation of the rights of all Negro applicants.

But it may be that in this respect the colleges simply cannot be compared with the schools. Thus, it might be pointed out: Attendance at universities is voluntary. Admission of students is achieved on an individualized basis, and the abolition of racial exclusion will not seriously affect this process except, perhaps, to increase the number of applications to be processed. But there are none of the problems which ensue from the duty to allocate students to a particular school. Nor are there problems of redistricting. And finally, since the students are supposedly more mature, the institutions may be thought to be better equipped to adjust to mixed attendance without serious friction.

Other circumstances may also make universities particularly vulnerable to lawsuit. Suits can be brought by individual Negro applicants seeking admission; there is no need for resort to the cumbersome "class action" (multiple plaintiff) type of suit which was utilized by the Negro plaintiffs in the school cases. Thus the suit is easy to initiate. It would also be harder to defend, for a suit by a single Negro plaintiff for admission to a college partakes of fewer of the grounds to justify delay in framing relief which are present in cases involving the schools.

6. Treatment of Integrated Students

Once Negro students are admitted to schools with white students, a question may arise as to whether state officials, in a sincere desire to avoid the possibilities of interracial friction, may take steps to avoid, as much as possible, contacts and intermingling between white and colored students in the schools. To be specific:

Can separate washrooms be provided?

Can separate lunch tables be provided?

Can the students be divided into separate class sections?

Can separate seating arrangements be utilized?

In a case involving a Negro student admitted to an Oklahoma university, the Court has already treated this issue. The precise question was whether the school authorities could accord "different treatment" to the Negro student "solely because of his race." The answer was a clear-cut "no." The "no" covered questions as to the legality of assignment of the Negro student to a special section of the classroom, a special table in the library and a special table in the lunchroom.

The Court admitted judicial impotence to deal with discriminations by other students. Social affairs are different; indeed, requiring social acceptance and social intermingling is far beyond the purview of the law. But, said the late Chief Justice Vinson: "There is a vast difference—a constitutional difference—between restrictions imposed by the state which prohibit the intellectual commingling of students, and the refusal of individuals to commingle where the state presents no bar." That principle would seem to have obvious application to mixed attendance in the schools. Constitutional prohibitions against restraints upon "intellectual commingling" may mean that all students regardless of race should have the same access to all advantages offered by the school.

Of course there may be special cases permitting some modification of the above.

Thus, some schools might wish to conduct separate classes for some or all students of a particular race where it becomes evident that these students are insufficiently prepared, by way of previous training and academic background, to participate with students of the other race. The principle enunciated in the Oklahoma case does not necessarily forbid recourse to such steps where the need for separation on scholastic grounds is demonstrable.

Again, appropriate measures—involving no racial differentiation—can obviously be taken to protect the health of all students. Nor should school authorities make the assumption that their hands are tied to the extent that they cannot take steps to forestall situations which present a patent danger of disorder. Enforced separation of pupils who attend the same classes in the same school "solely because of race" and for no other purpose would seem illegal; but reasonable regulations to secure discipline, health and scholastic improvement may be legal. These distinctions can surely be made if the reasons for making them are predicated on common sense and good faith and not subterfuge.

7. Revision of Existing Law

The North Carolina Constitution and the North Carolina Statutes contain provisions requiring separate schools for Negroes, white people, and Indians. As a result of the Supreme Court decision these provisions are in conflict with the Federal Constitution—the highest law of the land. The decisions of the Supreme Court defining rights under the Federal Constitution, like the Constitution itself, have the force of law. No repeal of the State's constitutional and statutory provisions is necessary before the rights enunciated by the Court in the segregation cases can be enforced.

But as a practical matter it would seem that if the State is to proceed in the business of gradual adjustment according to any policy which would allow considerable discretion at the local level and still permit proper supervision at the state level, then provision must be made for the exercise and distribution of such powers by new legislation. The alternative—no legislation—might invite confusion or chaos because it would invite diverse and conflicting action at the local level as well as litigation challenging the power of local boards to take any action without authorization from a higher authority.

The discussion in this paper has suggested—very roughly—some of the legal criteria for a system of "gradual adjustment" which might meet the requirements of the Brown decision.

If "gradual adjustment" becomes the law of the land, a need may exist to pass legislation to instruct the responsible educational authorities, by establishing broad authorization to take appropriate action, by defining general standards as to how and when to act, and by establishing a division of the powers to be exercised as between state and local officials.

Summary and Comment

After the Supreme Court renders its next decision, North Carolina schools will probably be bound by law to take steps to meet the constitutional prohibition against segregation.

Failure to do so will probably make the responsible school officials liable to suits by Negro parents seeking to secure the constitutional rights of their children. Of course, it would be impossible for a single group of Negroes, in a single law suit, to compel the State Board of Education to do something to de-segregate all schools in the State. Presumably, the State Board would never be subject to the jurisdiction of the courts except insofar as it made any attempt to exercise its power to prohibit local boards to make any effort to meet the requirements of the law. But suits could be lodged against the local boards. Moreover, these would not necessarily be actions by individual Negroes to enforce the rights of individual students. "Class actions" could be framed; in a single unit, groups of parents could join together, sue a local board and compel appropriate action to be taken in each of the schools which were subject to its jurisdiction. Thus, by the filing of a single complaint the entire school system of a county or a city might be brought under the purview of the injunctive power of a federal court. Indeed, a series of such class actions against local boards could be initiated by a single group of attorneys, and these cases might well be joined together for purposes of trial. Thus, with relatively little expense to the individual plaintiffs, and with relatively little effort as far as legal services are concerned, a group of Negroes could subject the operations of a large group of schools to the jurisdiction of the courts. Furthermore, outright purposeful refusal to make any effort to adjust to the law might also subject school officials to damage suits; and in especially flagrant cases, there even exists the possibility of criminal liability.

Damage suits, court supervision—this would hardly be a desirable situation. Coercion of school officials is to be deplored. Judicial intervention in the operation of the schools runs counter to deeply ingrained traditions of the American system of government. Flouting the law, especially when that law is the Constitution of the United States, is hardly a desirable course, especially in these troubled times.

The discussion in this study has been directed to the legal merit of various alternative courses—other than outright defiance. Doubts have been cast upon some proposals which contemplate total, permanent segregation. That does not, of course, prevent their adoption as calculated risks or as devices for delay and postponement of de-segregation. But perhaps even their value in that respect must be weighed against the possibility of subjecting the operation of

schools in North Carolina to litigious harassment, damage suits and considerable court supervision. And surely these alternatives must be weighed against a system of orderly, slow adjustment which might entail a minimum of court interference and a minimum of sudden change—especially in those areas where change is particularly difficult. This might also serve to "localize" the problems created by the *Brown* decision and thus reduce their proportions.

The legal basis for such an adjustment has been outlined. Principles were set forth relating to the time element, discretion, and the authority of school officials to cope with communities where serious racial antipathies exist, or with poorly backgrounded students. Principles were set forth relating to permissible ways of school placement, such as, use of attendance areas, assignment or election of schools by students. These principles are not now the law. But the discussion was aimed to prove that they might become the law. If North Carolina should decide that they would be useful, it has the power to urge the Supreme Court to recognize them; and, as shown, the Court might well respond favorably.

Of course, North Carolina is not obliged to appear before the Court next term. A variety of reasons might impel the State to shun the Court. But it is well to reiterate that the second decision may prove almost as important as the first. The Court has

plainly indicated an intent to establish law which will fix a pattern for compliance—a pattern which may apply, not just to Clarendon County, South Carolina, and to Prince Edward County, Virginia, but throughout the South. Thus the decision may be the guide which courts in North Carolina must follow in the future.

This State has a stake in the future course of the five segregation cases, and it is at least questionable that North Carolina's interests would be adequately represented by other parties to the litigation. There is no guarantee that others will conceive or satisfactorily demonstrate the case for a pattern of adjustment which will best fit the needs of this State. But this is not to suggest that the State must now commit itself to any fixed and detailed plan. On the contrary, it need commit itself to nothing. It need only explore the possibilities for action, examine the possible general principles relating to the "law of compliance," and ask the Court to sanction those principles which may appear to the State to be both feasible and legal. Such a step would leave open a course for total freedom of action in the future. It would also be consistent with a purpose which, after all, should pervade among the people of the State no matter what is done, a purpose to preserve respect for law, and especially that law which is organic—the Constitution of the United States.

Part III. The Text of the Court's Decisions

BROWN v. BOARD OF EDUCATION OF TOPEKA, 74 S.CT. 686 (1954)

[Opinion of the Supreme Court of the United States on the Seventeenth of May, 1954.]

WARREN, C. J.: These cases come to us from the States of Kansas, South Carolina, Virginia, and Delaware. They are premised on different facts and different local conditions, but a common legal question justifies their consideration together in this consolidated opinion.

In each of the cases, minors of the Negro race, through their legal representatives, seek the aid of the courts in obtaining admission to the public schools of their community on a non-segregated basis. In each instance, they had been denied admission to schools attended by white children under laws requiring or permitting segregation according to race. This segregation was alleged to deprive the plaintiffs of the equal protection of the laws under the Fourteenth Amendment. In each of the cases other than the Delaware case, a three-judge federal district court denied relief to the plaintiffs on the so-called "separate but equal" doctrine announced by this Court in *Plessy v. Ferguson*, 163 U.S. 537. Under that doctrine, equality of treatment is accorded when the races are provided substantially equal facilities, even though these facilities be separate. In the Delaware case, the Supreme Court of Delaware adhered to that doctrine, but ordered that the plaintiffs be admitted to the white schools because of their superiority to the Negro schools.

The plaintiffs contend that segregated public schools are not "equal" and cannot be made "equal," and that hence they are deprived of the equal protection of the laws. . . . Because of the obvious importance of the question presented, the Court took jurisdiction. Argument was heard in the 1952 Term, and reargument was heard this Term on certain questions propounded by the Court.

Reargument was largely devoted to the circumstances surrounding the adoption of the Fourteenth Amendment in 1868. It covered exhaustively consideration of the Amendment in Congress, ratification by the states, then existing practices in racial segregation, and the views of proponents and opponents of the Amendment. This discussion and our own investigation convince us that, although these sources cast some light, it is not enough to resolve the problem with which we are faced. At best, they are inconclusive. The most avid proponents of the post-War Amendments undoubtedly intended them to remove all legal distinctions among "all persons born or naturalized in the United States." Their opponents, just as certainly, were antagonistic to both the letter and the spirit of the Amendments and wished them to have the most limited effect. What others in Congress and the state legislatures had in mind cannot be determined with any degree of certainty.

An additional reason for the inconclusive nature of the Amendment's history, with respect to segregated schools, is the status of public education at that time. In the South, the movement toward free common schools, supported by general taxation, had not yet taken hold. Education of white children was largely in the hands of private groups. Education of Negroes was almost nonexistent, and practically all of the race were illiterate. In fact, any education of Negroes was forbidden by law in some states. Today, in contrast, many Negroes have achieved outstanding success in the arts and sciences as well as in the business and professional world. It is true that public education had already advanced further in the North, but the effect of the Amendment on Northern States was generally ignored in the congressional debates. Even in the North, the conditions of public education did not approximate those existing today. The curriculum was usually rudimentary; u n g r a d e d schools were common in rural areas; the school term was but three months a year in many states; and compulsory school attendance was virtually unknown. As a consequence, it is not surprising that there should be so little in the history of the Fourteenth Amendment relating to its intended effect on public education.

In the first cases in this Court construing the Fourteenth Amendment, decided shortly after its adoption, the Court interpreted it as proscribing all state-imposed discriminations against the Negro race. The doctrine of "separate but equal" did not make its appearance in this Court until 1896 in the case of Plessy v. Ferguson, supra, involving not education but transportation. American courts have since labored with the doctrine for over half a century. In this Court, there have been six cases

involving the "separate but equal" doctrine in the field of public education. In Cumming v. County Board of Education, 175 U.S. 528, and Gong Lum v. Rice, 275 U.S. 78, the validity of the doctrine itself was not challenged. In more recent cases, all on the graduate school level, inequality was found in that specific benefits enjoyed by white students were denied to Negro students of the same educational qualifications. Missouri ex rel. Gaines v. Canada, 305 U.S. 337; Sipuel v. Oklahoma, 332 U.S. 631; Sweatt v. Painter, 339 U.S. 629; McLaurin v. Oklahoma State Regents, 339 U.S. 637. In none of these cases was it necessary to reexamine the doctrine to grant relief to the Negro plaintiff. And in Sweatt v. Painter, supra, the Court expressly reserved decision on the question whether Plessy v. Ferguson should be held inapplicable to public education.

In the instant cases, that question is directly presented. Here, unlike Sweatt v. Painter, there are findings below that the Negro and white schools involved have been equalized, or are being equalized, with respect to buildings, curricula, qualifications and salaries of teachers, and other "tangible" factors. Our decision, therefore, cannot turn on merely a comparison of these tangible factors in the Negro and white schools involved in each of the cases. We must look instead to the effect of segregation itself on public education.

In approaching this problem, we cannot turn the clock back to 1868 when the Amendment was adopted, or even to 1896 when Plessy v. Ferguson was written. We must consider public education in the light of its full development and its present place in American life throughout the Nation. Only in this way can it be determined if segregation in public schools deprives these plaintiffs of the equal protection of the laws.

Today, education is perhaps the most important function of state and local governments. Compulsory school attendance laws and the great expenditures for education both demonstrate our recognition of the importance of education to our democratic society. It is required in the performance of our most basic public responsibilities, even service in the armed forces. It is the very foundation of good citizenship. Today it is a principal instrument in awakening the child to cultural values, in preparing him for later professional training, and in helping him to adjust normally to his environment. In

these days, it is doubtful that any child may reasonably be expected to succeed in life if he is denied the opportunity of an education. Such an opportunity, where the state has undertaken to provide it, is a right which must be made available to all on equal terms.

We come then to the question presented: Does segregation of children in public schools solely on the basis of race, even though the physical facilities and other "tangible" factors may be equal, deprive the children of the minority group of equal educational opportunities? We believe that it does.

In Sweatt v. Painter, supra, in finding that a segregated law school for Negroes could not provide them equal educational opportunities, this Court relied in large part on "those qualities which are incapable of objective measurement but which make for greatness in a law school." McLaurin v. Oklahoma State Regents, supra, the Court, in requiring that a Negro admitted to a white graduate school be treated like all other students, again resorted to intangible considerations: ". . . his ability to study, to engage in discussions and exchange views with other students, and, in general, to learn his profession." Such considerations apply with added force to children in grade and high schools. To separate them from others of similar age and qualifications solely because of their race generates a feeling of inferiority as to their status in the community that may affect their hearts and minds in a way unlikely ever to be undone. The effect of this separation on their educational opportunities was well stated by a finding in the Kansas case by a court which nevertheless felt compelled to rule against the Negro plaintiffs:

"Segregation of white and colored children in public schools has a detrimental effect upon the colored children. The impact is greater when it has the sanction of the law; for the policy of separating the races is usually interpreted as denoting the inferiority of the Negro group. A sense of inferiority affects the motivation of a child to learn. Segregation with the sanction of law, therefore, has a tendency to retard the educational and mental development of Negro children and to deprive them of some of the benefits they would receive in a racially integrated school system."

Whatever may have been the extent of psychological knowledge at the time of Plessy v. Ferguson, this finding is amply supported by modern authority. Any language in *Plessy* v. *Ferguson* contrary to this finding is rejected.

We conclude that in the field of public education the doctrine of "separate but equal" has no place. Separate educational facilities are inherently unequal. Therefore, we hold that the plaintiffs and others similarly situated for whom the actions have been brought are, by reason of the segregation complained of, deprived of the equal protection of the laws guaranteed by the Fourteenth Amendment. This disposition makes unnecessary any discussion whether such segregation also violates the Due Process Clause of the Fourteenth Amendment.

Because these are class actions, because of the wide applicability of this decision, and because of the great variety of local conditions, the formulation of decrees in these cases presents problems of considerable complexity. On reargument, the consideration of appropriate relief was necessarily subordinated to the primary question—the constitutionality of segregation in public education. We have now announced that such segregation is a denial of the equal protection of the laws. In order that we may have the full assistance of the parties in formulating decrees, the cases will be restored to the docket, and the parties are requested to present further argument on Questions 4 and 5 previously propounded by the Court for the reargument this Term. The Attorney General of the United States is again invited to participate. The Attorneys General of the states requiring or permitting segregation in public education will also be permitted to appear as *amici curiae* upon request to do so by September 15, 1954, and submission of briefs by October 1, 1954.

BOLLING v. SHARPE, 74 S. CT. 693 (1954)

[Opinion of the Supreme Court of the United States on the Seventeenth of May, 1954.]

WARREN, C. J.: This case challenges the validity of segregation in the public schools of the District of Columbia. The petitioners, minors of the Negro race, allege that such segregation deprives them of due process of law under the Fifth Amendment. They were refused admission to a public school attended by white children solely because of their race. They sought the aid of the District Court for the District of Columbia in obtaining admission. That court dismissed their complaint. We granted a writ of certiorari before judgment in the Court of Appeals because of the importance of the constitutional question presented.

We have this day held that the Equal Protection Clause of the Fourteenth Amendment prohibits the states from maintaining racially segregated public schools. The legal problem in the District of Columbia is somewhat different, however. The Fifth Amendment, which is applicable in the District of Columbia, does not contain an equal protection clause as does the Fourteenth Amendment which applies only to the states. But the concepts of equal protection and due process, both stemming from our American ideal of fairness, are not mutually exclusive. The "equal protection of the laws" is a more explicit safeguard of prohibited unfairness than "due process of law," and, therefore, we do not imply that the two are always interchangeable phrases. But, as this Court has recognized, discrimination may be so unjustifiable as to be violative of due process.

Classifications based solely upon race must be scrutinized with par-

ticular care, since they are contrary to our traditions and hence constitutionally suspect. As long ago as 1896, this Court declared the principle "that the Constitution of the United States, in its present form, forbids, so far as civil and political rights are concerned, discrimination by the General Government, or by the States, against any citizen because of his race." And in *Buchanan* v. *Warley*, 245 U.S. 60, the Court held that a statute which limited the right of a property owner to convey his property to a person of another race was, as an unreasonable discrimination, a denial of due process of law.

Although the Court has not assumed to define "liberty" with any great precision, that term is not confined to mere freedom from bodily restraint. Liberty under law extends to the full range of conduct which the individual is free to pursue, and it cannot be restricted except for a proper governmental objective. Segregation in public education is not reasonably related to any proper governmental objective, and thus it imposes on Negro children of the District of Columbia a burden that constitutes an arbitrary deprivation of their liberty in violation of the Due Process Clause.

In view of our decision that the Constitution prohibits the states from maintaining racially segregated public schools, it would be unthinkable that the same Constitution would impose a lesser duty on the Federal Government. We hold that racial segregation in the public schools of the District of Columbia is a denial of the due process of law guaranteed by the Fifth Amendment to the Constitution.

For the reasons set out in *Brown* v. *Board of Education*, this case will be restored to the docket for reargument on Questions 4 and 5 previously propounded by the Court.

States by Percentage of Negro Population, 1950

State	Total Population	% Negro	% White	% Other Races
Mississippi	2,178,914	45.27	54.55	.17
South Carolina	2,117,027	38.83	61.10	.07
District of Columbia	802,178	35.01	64.55	.44
Louisiana	2,683,516	32.88	66.95	.16
Alabama	3,061,743	32.00	67.92	.08
Georgia	3,444,578	30.85	69.11	.04
North Carolina	4,061,929	25.78	73.44	.77
Arkansas	1,909,511	22.34	77.59	.07
Virginia	3,318,680	22.12	77.79	.09
Florida	2,771,305	21.76	78.16	.08
Maryland	2,343,001	16.47	83.44	.09
Tennessee	3,291,718	16.12	83.85	.03
Delaware	318,085	13.71	86.10	.19
Texas	7,711,194	12.68	87.23	.09
Missouri	3,954,653	7.51	92.44	.05
Illinois	8,712,176	7.41	92.35	.23
Michigan	6,371,766	6.94	92.88	.18
Kentucky	2,944,806	6.86	93.12	.02
New Jersey	4,835,329	6.59	93.30	.11
Oklahoma	2,233,351	6.52	91.00	2.48
Ohio	7,946,627	6.45	93.48	.07
New York	14,830,192	6.19	93.54	.27
Pennsylvania	10,498,012	6.08	93.86	.05
West Virginia	2,005,552	5.73	94.25	.02
Indiana	3,934,224	4.43	95.53	.04
California	10,586,223	4.37	93.66	1.97
Kansas	1,905,299	3.84	95.99	.17
Arizona	749,587	3.46	87.32	9.22
Nevada	160,083	2.69	93.64	3.67
Connecticut	2,007,280	2.66	97.26	.07
Rhode Island	791,896	1.76	98.12	.12
Massachusetts	4,690,514	1.56	98.32	.12
Colorado	1,325,089	1.52	97.85	.62
Nebraska	1,325,510	1.45	98.18	.37
Washington	2,378,963	1.29	97.37	1.34
New Mexico	681,178	1.23	92.52	6.25
Wyoming	290,529	0.88	97.76	1.36
Wisconsin	3,434,575	0.82	98.78	.40
Oregon	1,521,341	0.76	98.41	.83
Iowa	2,621,073	0.75	99.18	.07
Minnesota	2,982,483	0.47	99.03	.50
Utah	688,862	0.40	98.26	1.34
Montana	591,024	0.21	96.79	3.00
Idaho	588,637	0.18	98.77	1.05
New Hampshire	533,242	0.14	99.82	.04
Maine	913,774	0.13	99.68	.19
Vermont	377,747	0.12	99.85	.03
South Dakota	652,740	0.11	96.29	3.60
North Dakota	619,636	0.04	98.19	1.76

Source: Population data from the U. S. Bureau of the Census, 1950.

University of North Carolina
Chapel Hill

The Institute of Government grew out of the classroom of a teacher in the Law School of the University of North Carolina in the 1920's. It developed into a program of action supported by city, county, state, and federal officials in North Carolina during the 1930's. It became an integral part of the structure of the University of North Carolina in January, 1942.

The Institute of Government unites public officials, private citizens, and students and teachers of civics and government in a systematic effort to meet definite and practical needs in North Carolina.

(1) It seeks to coordinate the efforts and activities of city, county, state, and federal officials who have been working for one hundred and fifty years on the same problems, for the same people, in the same territory, in overlapping governmental units, without coming together in systematic and continued cooperative effort—in the effort to eliminate needless duplication, friction, and waste.

(2) It seeks to bridge the gap between outgoing and incoming officials at the end of their two- or four-year terms by organizing and transmitting our steadily accumulating governmental experience to successive generations of public officials—in the effort to cut down the lost time, lost motion, and lost money involved in a rotating governmental personnel.

(3) It seeks to collect and correlate for each group of public officials the laws governing their powers and duties now scattered through a multiplicity of books to the point of practical inaccessibility in constitutional provisions, legislative enactments (including public-local and private laws), municipal ordinances, and court decisions—in the effort to make them conveniently available for practical use.

(4) It seeks to collect and compare the different methods of doing similar things rising out of the initiative and resourcefulness of officials in a hundred county courthouses, three hundred city halls, scores of state departments, and federal agencies—in the effort to raise the standards of governmental performance by lifting the poorest practices to the level of the best.

(5) It seeks to bridge the gap between government as it is taught in schools and as it is practiced in city halls, county courthouses, state departments, and federal agencies.

(6) It seeks to provide the machinery for putting the people in touch with their government and keeping them in touch with it.

(7) It seeks to build a demonstration laboratory and clearinghouse of governmental information to which successive generations of officials, citizens, students and teachers of government may go to see demonstrated in one place the methods and practices in government they would now have to go to one hundred counties, about three hundred cities and towns, and a score or more of state departments to find—and would not find practically available for use when they had reached these sources.

The Institute of Government is working with officials and citizens and the schools to achieve the foregoing objectives through comparative studies of the structure and workings of government in the cities, counties, and state of North Carolina, by staff members going from one city hall, county courthouse, state department, and federal agency to another, collecting, comparing, and classifying the laws and practices in books and in action. It is setting forth the results of these studies in guidebooks, demonstrating them in laboratories, teaching them in training schools, keeping them up to date, and transmitting them through a clearinghouse of governmental information for officials, citizens, and teachers of civics and government in the schools.

CPSIA information can be obtained
at www.ICGtesting.com
Printed in the USA
LVHW050031271118
598300LV00027B/1093/P